TECHNO-MATTER

THE MATERIALS BEHIND THE MARVELS

FRED BORTZ

TWENTY-FIRST CENTURY BOOKS
BROOKFIELD, CONNECTICUT

**To my sister, Fay Nedra Zachary,
for whom "Novel Materials" has quite a different meaning
FB**

Cover photography courtesy of Photo Researchers, Inc.
© Victor Habbick Visions/SPL

Photographs courtesy of Photo Researchers, Inc.: pp. 9 (© Mehau Kulyk/SPL), 11 (© Charles D. Winters), 12 (© Ken Eward/BioGrafx), 13 (© John Walsh/SPL), 20-21 (© Rafael Macia), 34 (© Astrid and Hanns-Frieder Michler/SPL), 36 (© Tek Image/SPL), 42 (right: © Laguna Design/SPL), 66 (© Ken Eward/BioGrafx), 69 (© Hank Morgan), 80 (© David Parker/SPL), 84 (© Doe); Peter Arnold, Inc.: pp. 13 (© Manfred Kage), 33 (© Leonard Lessin), 62 (© James L. Amos); © Tom Pantages: pp. 23, 24, 42 (left); Visuals Unlimited: pp. 25 (© Westinghouse), 57; Archive Photos: pp. 51, 54; UPI/Corbis-Bettmann: p. 73; Brown Brothers: p. 75; © Vince Streano/Corbis: p. 87

Library of Congress Cataloging-in-Publication Data
Bortz, Alfred, B.
Techno-matter : the materials behind the marvels / by Fred Bortz.
    p. cm.
  Includes bibliographical references and index.
  ISBN 0-7613-1469-5 (lib. bdg.)
  1. Materials. 2. Microstructure. 3. Synthetic products. I. Title.
  TA403.6. B68 2001
  620.1'1—dc21   00-034390

Published by Twenty-First Century Books
A Division of The Millbrook Press, Inc.
2 Old New Milford Road
Brookfield, Connecticut 06804
www.millbrookpress.com

CONTENTS

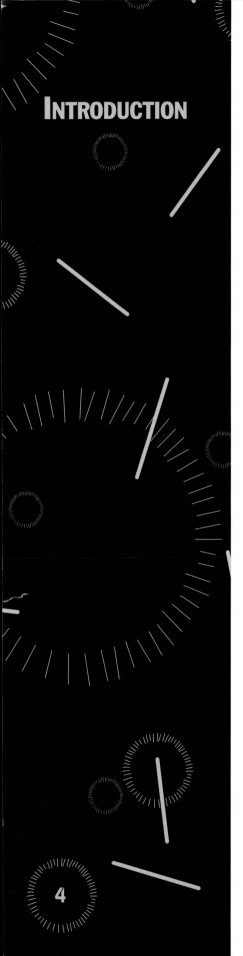

MARVELS AND MATERIALS

For as long as people have looked out into the universe, they have imagined what it might be like to live on other worlds. Today we have gone beyond imagination to planning. When you are an adult, you may be one of the designers, builders, or inhabitants of a human colony on the Moon or Mars. You may grow up to be one of the engineers, scientists, astronauts, or any of the many other important team members who take part in that great adventure.

To build and sustain a colony on Mars, the pioneers will have to learn to use Martian natural resources. It will be too difficult, expensive, and time consuming to bring everything from Earth. They will need to create a breathable atmosphere. They will need to build systems to collect and use Martian water. They will need to create a Martian ecology based on bacteria, plants, and animals from Earth.

They will need to build factories of many kinds. What will they make first: vehicles, computers, sources of electricity, communication systems? All of those will be necessary, but they will probably have a few of those from Earth to get started. If they want to build more on Mars, they'll need to make metals from Martian ores. They'll need to make ceramics, glass, and materials for electronic and electrical devices from Martian sand and soil. They'll need to find ways of growing or manufacturing the raw materials for plastic and synthetic fabrics.

Before they can make their day-to-day items, their machines, and their "high-technology" devices, they'll need to make the materials that will go into those things. They'll need far more to sustain human life on Mars than to get there. This book is the story not of the technology that will take us to Mars but rather of the field of science and engineering that will keep us there. That field gets far less public attention than the sciences you might study in high school (biology, chemistry, and physics) or the best-known branches of engineering that you might recognize as majors in college (civil, mechanical, electrical, and chemical).

This book is about materials science and engineering, a field so exciting and important that our grand technologies would not exist without it. Nature gives us natural resources. Materials scientists and engineers transform those resources into human-made materials. Perhaps people would pay more attention to those substances if they had a catchier name. That's why we chose the title *Techno-Matter: The Materials Behind the Marvels* for this book.

Because of materials science and engineering, more marvels of technology lie ahead. Whether you live all your life on Earth or some of it on other worlds, you will see astonishing things. We can't predict exactly what those will be, but of this we can be certain: Human technology will rely, then as now, on substances that are better than those nature can ever make. They may be plastics, synthetic fabrics, metallic alloys, ceramics, semiconductors, superconductors, superadhesives, supermagnets, or combinations of those marvelous materials—or they may be substances we cannot yet even imagine.

Just remember this slogan when you're planning that trip to Mars. Techno-Matter: You can't leave home without it!

IT'S NOT MAGIC; IT'S MICRO-STRUCTURE

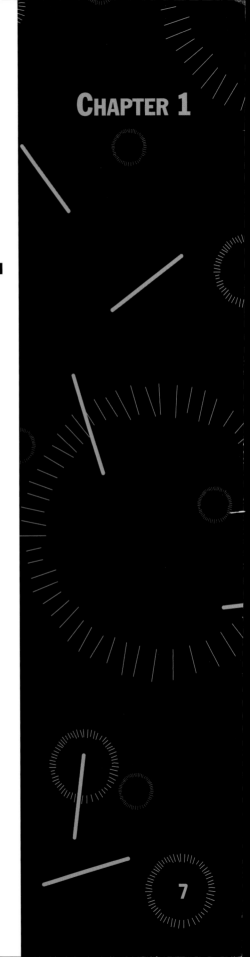

At the beginning of the twentieth century, astronomer Percival Lowell, studying Mars from his private observatory in Flagstaff, Arizona, was convinced that the planet supported intelligent life. One hundred years later, we know that Lowell was wrong—or perhaps we should say he was just premature. As the twenty-first century begins, many scientists and engineers are convinced that intelligent life—a permanent human colony—will be thriving on Mars in their lifetimes.

The great adventure will begin with a few pioneering men and women setting off on a spectacular voyage in spacecraft full of marvelous devices. Some people might even call it magical, but the scientists and engineers who design and build the spaceship and its equipment will know better. If they are materials scientists and engineers, they will know that behind the marvels lie human-made materials far better than nature provides. We might call their creations Techno-Matter.

What do we mean when we call a substance a material? A material is a substance—usually a solid—that we choose because it behaves in a particular way under particular conditions. We describe that behavior as a "property."

For example, some materials are hard, and others are soft. Some are heavy, and others are light. Some materials bend gradually, and others resist a force until they snap. Light passes through some materials, reflects from others, and is absorbed by still others.

Some materials can become powerful magnets, and others are barely affected by the strongest magnets. Some materials allow electricity or heat to travel through them easily. Others resist the flow of electricity, heat, or both. Some materials melt at a low temperature, but others remain solid in the hottest furnaces. Some materials are smooth, but other materials are rough or sticky. Some materials can be sliced very thinly, but others crumble instead.

What makes the properties of one material different from all others? The difference begins with the very tiny particles called atoms and molecules that make up all matter, but it doesn't end there. A material's properties come not only from its atoms or molecules but also from the way in which they are arranged.

If a substance has only one kind of atom, we call it an element. Nature has given us fewer than one hundred different elements on Earth. You probably recognize the names of many of the most useful or common ones, such as (in alphabetical order) aluminum, calcium, carbon, chlorine, copper, gold, helium, hydrogen, iron, lead, mercury, neon, nickel, nitrogen, oxygen, phosphorus, platinum, potassium, silicon, silver, sodium, sulfur, and uranium.

H 1																	He 2
Li 3	Be 4											B 5	C 6	N 7	O 8	F 9	Ne 10
Na 11	Mg 12											Al 13	Si 14	P 15	S 16	Cl 17	Ar 18
K 19	Ca 20	Sc 21	Ti 22	U 23	Cr 24	Mn 25	Fe 26	Co 27	Ni 28	Cu 29	Zn 30	Ga 31	Ge 32	As 33	Se 34	Br 35	Kr 36
Rb 37	Sr 38	Y 39	Zr 40	Nb 41	Mo 42	Tc 43	Ru 44	Rh 45	Pd 46	Ag 47	Cd 48	In 49	Sn 50	Sb 51	Te 52	I 53	Xe 54
Cs 55	Ba 56		Hf 72	Ta 73	W 74	Re 75	Os 76	Ir 77	Pt 78	Au 79	Hg 80	Tl 81	Pb 82	Bi 83	Po 84	At 85	Rn 86
Fr 87	Ra 88		Rf 104	Ha 105	Sg 106	Ns 107	Hs 108	Mt 109									

La 57	Ce 58	Pr 59	Nd 60	Pm 61	Sm 62	Eu 63	Gd 64	Tb 65	Dy 66	Ho 67	Er 68	Tm 69	Yb 70	Lu 71
Ac 89	Th 90	Pa 91	U 92	Np 93	Pu 94	Am 95	Cm 96	Bk 97	Cf 98	Es 99	Fm 100	Md 101	No 102	Lw 103

The periodic table shows the known elements arranged in order of their atomic numbers (the number of protons in the atomic nucleus). Elements with similar chemistry occur in the same vertical column. Different groups of elements are color coded. From left: alkaline metals (orange-yellow); transition metals (magenta-blue); semimetals and nonmetals (green-orange); noble gases (dark blue). Hydrogen stands alone at the top, and along the bottom are the lanthanide series (magenta-green) and the actinide series (magenta-orange.) Periodic tables help scientists predict how an element will behave chemically, and how the atoms of different elements combine together in molecules.

Atoms often join together in specific combinations that we call molecules. When a substance is made of only one kind of molecule, we call it a compound. For example, the most important compound for life is water. A molecule of water forms when two hydrogen atoms and one oxygen atom combine.

Although it seems odd, two or more materials can be made of exactly the same atoms or molecules and have very different properties. For example, diamond, the hardest material in nature, and graphite, so soft and slippery that it is used in pencil "leads" and as a lubricant, are both carbon. How can that be?

The answer lies in the "microstructure," or the arrangement of the joined atoms, of the two materials. The atoms of a solid usually connect to each other in a repeating pattern known as a crystal structure. The connection between two atoms is called a bond. Depending on the kind of atoms or molecules involved, each one can have several bonds to its neighbors in the crystal. The bonds have a particular length and arrangement around the atom. It takes energy to change the length of bonds or the angles between them. Carbon atoms generally form four bonds.

In the diamond crystal structure (see the diagram on page 11), each carbon atom sits in the middle of a pyramid-like shape called a "tetrahedron," bonded to four other carbon atoms at the corners. No matter which way you try to push on that three-dimensional structure, you end up trying to squeeze some bonds, stretch others, and change the angles between them. That makes the diamond very hard.

As the diagram on page 12 shows, graphite is very different. Its microstructure is like an evenly spaced stack of chicken wire. Each carbon atom is bonded strongly to three

Diamond is a form of carbon in which each atom is connected to four others in a three-dimensional structure. It is a very hard material because no matter in which direction you push, your effort is opposed by a strong bond.

others in its two-dimensional layer. Its fourth bond is split equally between the two layers above and below it, and is therefore quite weak. By pushing or pulling two neighboring layers in opposite directions, it is easy to break those weak bonds and slide the layers across one another. That's what makes graphite soft and slippery.

When you think of diamonds, you probably think of carefully cut and polished glittering gemstones; but most diamonds are small impure fragments. A collection of these very hard and sharp fragments, known as "bort" or "bortz" to the amusement of the author, is quite useful for industrial processes such as grinding and polishing.

diamond atom structure

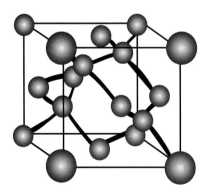

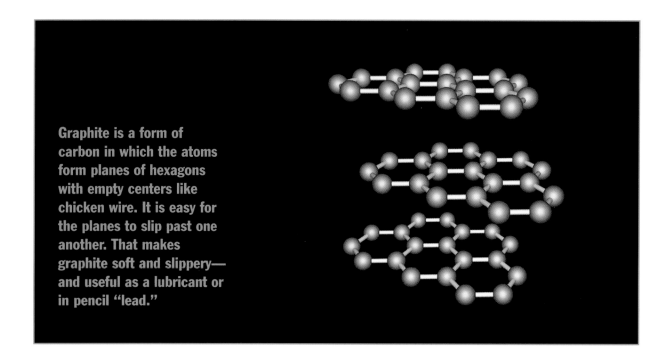

Graphite is a form of carbon in which the atoms form planes of hexagons with empty centers like chicken wire. It is easy for the planes to slip past one another. That makes graphite soft and slippery—and useful as a lubricant or in pencil "lead."

graphite atom structure

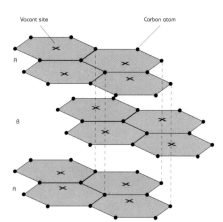

Vacant site   Carbon atom

A

B

A

Still, it's the gemstones that get your attention. You might think that clear glass or ice cut into the same shape and size would sparkle as much as a diamond, but that is not so. Not only is diamond the hardest known material it also bends, or refracts, light more than any other clear substance. A cut diamond's shape and the way it refracts light determine its sparkle. The larger it is and the more it sparkles, the greater its value.

A diamond's microstructure is also important to its value as a gem. The more perfect the arrangement of atoms in the crystal, the more clear the diamond appears. Sometimes a diamond can have microscopic bits of graphite inside. If a jeweler can see those, the diamond's value as a gem is much less. However, certain kinds of imperfection can actually make some gemstones more valuable. A scattering of certain

"impurities" (atoms of a kind that don't belong in the pure substance) throughout a gemstone's crystal structure can sometimes change its color slightly but dramatically.

Diamonds are also valuable because they are rare on Earth—at least in the parts of the planet where people can get to them. Carbon takes the form of diamond only under conditions of high pressure and high temperature such as those found deep under the Earth's surface. Geologic activity brings some diamonds up to where we can mine them, but most are forever out of our reach.

Just as nature has created both diamond and graphite microstructures from carbon, materials scientists and engineers have learned to work wonders with microstructure. Their work has created the marvelous materials behind today's high-tech wonders, and it will carry us beyond tomorrow's dreams.

Some people are tempted to call those creations magical, but materials scientists and engineers know better. In their world of Techno-Matter, they would simply declare, "It's not magic; it's microstructure!" and then go back to work.

Diamond refracts light more than any other clear material. This colorful polarized-light image takes advantage of that property to show the tensions within the gemstone's crystal structure.

Many gemstones are made of the mineral corundum, or aluminum oxide, with slight differences in impurities leading to different colors. This blue stone is a sapphire. Other forms of corundum are ruby (red), oriental topaz (yellow), amethyst (violet), and oriental emerald (green).

THE IMPORTANCE OF IMPERFECTION

People usually notice that a material is crystalline because it has precise shapes, like the right-angle edges of rock salt, or because it cuts more easily along certain planes than others, like gemstones. They sometimes think that glass is crystalline because it can be cut to look like a crystal (in fact, fine-cut glassware is often called "crystal"), but glass—as you will discover later—is not a crystal at all.

People rarely think of metals or ceramics as crystals, yet many important properties of those materials are determined by their crystalline nature—including their imperfections. Any large crystal has its share of imperfections or defects. With billions of billions of molecules in something as small as a snowflake, absolute perfection of any crystal is more than nature or the best of human technology can achieve. In fact, absolute perfection of a crystal is usually less desirable than controlled imperfection. Later chapters will tell you why that is so. For now, let's look at the different types of imperfections in crystals.

Grains

Most solid substances are crystalline, but only a few of them ever form crystals large enough for people to notice. The rest are made up of many tiny crystal regions. Each tiny crystal region is called a "grain." Each grain has the same properties as any other, and if you were to examine the individual atoms in a grain, you would find them lined up in crystal planes with the same pattern and spacing as the atoms in any other grain. But if you were to compare two neighboring grains, you would find that their crystal planes did not line up with each other.

Point Defects

The pattern of atoms or molecules in a crystal is called a crystal lattice, and each position in that arrangement is called a lattice site. If you think of a crystal as a baseball stadium, the lattice is the evenly spaced arrangement of seats, and each seat is a lattice site. A perfect crystal is an arrangement of atoms on that lattice in a repeating pattern that is perfectly predictable. For example, a perfect sodium chloride crystal would be like a man in each even-numbered seat and a woman in each odd-numbered seat in one row and the opposite arrangement of the sexes in the next row.

Now if someone stays home, or if a lattice site is unoccupied, we have a point defect called a "vacancy." If someone sneaks into the stadium and squeezes in between two seats by standing on the arm rest, or if an extra atom or molecule squeezes into the crystal where there is no lattice site for it, we have a different kind of point defect called an "interstitial." If a Martian steals someone's ticket and uses the seat, or if an atom of potassium is present where a sodium atom belongs, that point defect is called an "impurity."

A point defect affects the properties of the crystal not only at that lattice site but also nearby. Atoms shift a bit to fill in some of the space left by a vacancy. An interstitial atom pushes nearby atoms a bit out of place, and those atoms push their neighbors, and so forth. An impurity can cause either of those effects, depending on whether it is larger or smaller than the atom it replaces. Or it can cause even more dramatic effects. A Martian in a stadium would certainly attract reporters to its area. Impurities in aluminum oxide give ruby and sapphire their distinctive colors, and carefully placed impurities turn silicon into transistors.

Many properties of materials are determined by imperfections in their crystal structure. The upper diagram shows two point defects, a vacancy and an interstitial. The lower diagram shows a line defect, or dislocation.

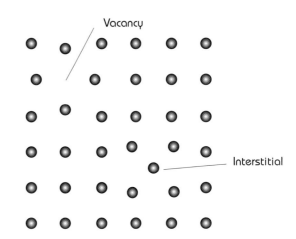

Vacancy

Interstitial

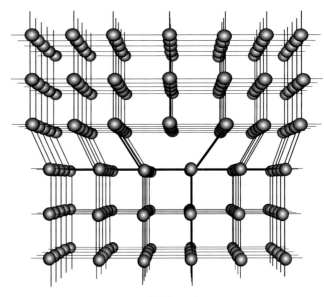

Dislocation

Line Defects

A dislocation, or line defect, occurs when the atomic planes of one section of a crystal lattice are lined up but slightly offset from another. When scientists discovered dislocations, they finally began to understand what happens when they "work" metals. For example, bronze hardens when it is beaten. That happens because its dislocations move until they reach a place in the crystal where their further movement is blocked.

Planar Defects

Two types of imperfections fall into the category of planar defects. One of these is a grain boundary, where two grains come together. There the crystal lattice planes of the two grains do not line up. The other type of planar defect occurs in crystals that have different atomic arrangements in neighboring planes. The different planes normally follow one another in a repeating sequence. For example, three planes might repeat in ABC-ABC-ABC order. Occasionally, a plane might be missing (ABC-AB-ABC) or misplaced (ABC-ACB-ABC). When that happens, the crystal is said to have a stacking fault.

Volume Defects

A volume defect, usually called an inclusion, is a small region of the crystal that is entirely different from its surroundings. It may be a large number of molecules or atoms of the same impurity, or it may be another crystalline form of the same substance. For example, diamonds often have inclusions of graphite, which greatly diminish their value as gems, but not their hardness. Those are useful as industrial diamonds, as noted on page 11.

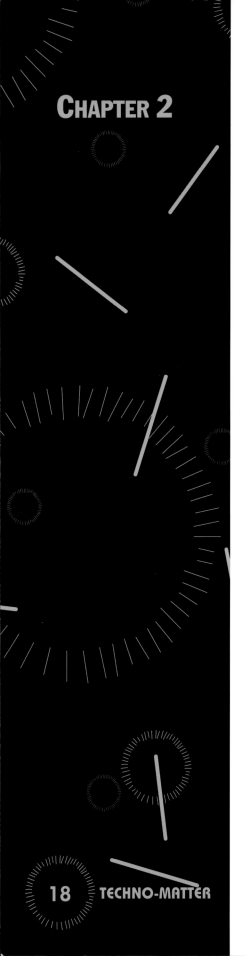

CHAPTER 2

ELECTRO-MATTER

It's a stormy morning, and the clock radio wakes you for school. You turn on the lamp and crawl out of bed. The buzz in the bathroom tells you that your big sister is shaving her legs.

You pound on the door. "Hey, it's my turn!" you complain. "You should've done that last night."

"Be patient," she whines. "I'll be out as soon as I dry my hair."

You reply with a special insult you had saved for the occasion, but the whir of the hair dryer drowns you out. Grumbling, you head for the kitchen. You get some waffles out of the freezer and pop them into the toaster. Its coils glow red. You put some hot chocolate mix into a cup, add water, put it into the microwave oven, and push a few buttons.

By the time your sister dashes in, you're eating breakfast and the sound of your favorite group, the Beethoven Blasters, is blaring from the CD player. Your sister hates them. "That's what you get for hogging the bathroom," you say with a grin.

She shows you a computer diskette and holds it just out of your reach. "And this is what you get for hogging the computer," she snarls. Your multimedia presentation for science class is on that disk. How could you have forgotten to take it out of the disk drive? She hands you "Mangled Mozart" by Danny and the Declassifiers. "If you ever want to see this diskette again, take that CD out and put this one in," she orders.

"One of these days, I'll show you," you threaten as you take the CD and diskette from her hands. "Just for one day, I wish you would have to live without your razor, your hair dryer, your CD player, and your computer." Suddenly, a lightning bolt flashes across the dark sky, and a crash of thunder shakes the house. The lights flicker, and then the power goes out.

"What did you say?" your sister asks, eyes widening. "I wonder how long this will last."

"Maybe for a whole day," you gloat. "At least I've had my breakfast."

CONDUCTORS, INSULATORS, AND SEMICONDUCTORS

What if the electric power would go off for a whole day, not just in your home but everywhere else in your town? You'd certainly discover how important electricity is in today's world. Still, you would probably never stop to think of the materials that make it all possible—unless you had read this chapter. Over the next few pages, you'll read the inside story of this electric world. You'll discover the Techno-Matter behind the electrical and electronic machines that we would never want to live without.

Of all the forms of energy that people use to run their machines, electrical energy is the most versatile and controllable. Electrical energy is carried by an electric current, or the

Modern city life would
not be the same without
electricity: no street-
lights or traffic lights or
neon signs; no elevated
railways or subways; no
elevators in tall build-
ings; no telephone,
radio, or television . . .

flow of electrical charges. Our electrical and electronic
machines depend on getting the electric charge to flow—or
not flow—exactly where we want it. To do that, we use different kinds of materials with different kinds of microstructures. We classify those as conductors, insulators, and
semiconductors, according to the way an electric charge
passes through them.

Electricity in Matter Electric forces create the bonds
between atoms in molecules or in a material. They also hold

each atom together. As tiny as an atom is, it contains even smaller particles held together by electricity.

To understand the electrical properties of materials, we have to begin with those smaller particles. Each atom has a central part called a nucleus. The nucleus contains most of the atom's mass and is made up of two kinds of particles, protons and neutrons. Each proton carries an electric charge of a type scientists call positive. Neutrons carry no electric charge. The number of protons determines the type of atom. Carbon, for example, has six protons in its nucleus.

Surrounding the nucleus like a cloud are very light particles called electrons. The electron cloud is several thousand times as large as the nucleus. If the nucleus were as big as a basketball, then the electron cloud would be a ball a mile across. Each electron carries the same amount of electrical charge as a proton, but of an opposite type that scientists call negative. An atom is electrically neutral, because it has the same number of positively charged protons and negatively charged electrons. For instance, an oxygen atom has eight protons and eight electrons. Adding charges of +8 and −8 gives zero.

When electrically charged bodies come close to each other, they pull on (attract) or push against (repel) each other. Pairs of like charges (both positive or both negative) repel, and pairs of unlike charges (one positive and one negative) attract. The closer together the charges are, the stronger the force between them. An atom stays together because its negatively charged electrons are attracted to its positively charged nucleus.

Because electrons are light and relatively far from the nucleus, the holding power of the electrical force is not always enough to keep every electron in its place. It isn't hard for one or two of the outer electrons to be pulled away from an atom. Likewise, it isn't hard for an atom to attract an extra one or two outer electrons. In many materials, neighboring atoms can share pairs of their outermost electrons. That sharing creates the bonds you read about in the previous chapter.

Electrical Conductivity and Resistance When electric charges move or flow from one place to another, scientists call that an electric current. In some materials, electricity flows

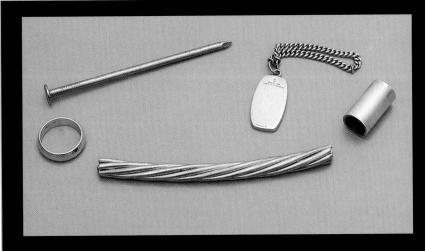

Metals conduct electricity well. Pictured here are some everyday items that would serve as excellent conductors: an iron nail, a gold ring, some braided copper wire, a keychain with a silver tag, and a small piece of aluminum tubing.

easily. They are said to be good conductors or to have high electrical conductivity. Other materials do not allow electric charges to flow easily. They are said to be poor conductors or to have high electrical resistance. If they block the flow of current almost completely, they are called insulators.

What makes one material a good conductor while another is an insulator? It is the atoms or molecules in the material and the way they are arranged. In other words, it is the microstructure.

Metals are excellent conductors of electricity. They carry an electric current easily, without much loss of energy. Each atom in a metal has electrons that it shares with all the other atoms in the crystal. Because those electrons are shared, they easily move from place to place. When their motion is in one direction more than another, the metal is carrying an electric current. For example, shared electrons flow in the copper wires that carry the electricity from your wall sockets to your

Many common materials are insulators, which means that they do not carry electricity well. Those include wood, rubber, plastic, glass, and fabric.

appliances. Those shared electrons are commonly called "conduction electrons."

In contrast, the rubbery material around household wires is a good insulator. It protects you from the electricity in the metal. Many materials besides rubber, including glass, ceramics, plastic, and fabrics, are also insulators. They block the flow of an electric current because they have almost no conduction electrons. Nearly every electron in an insulator is bound tightly to its atom and molecule, so it is very hard to drive an electric current through.

Semiconductors Materials called semiconductors also have high electrical resistance, but not nearly as high as insulators. They have a few conduction electrons, but not very many. It takes a lot of electrical pressure, called voltage, to drive an electric current through them. The most important electrical property of a semiconductor is not its conductivity, but rather the way that its conductivity changes under certain conditions. Small changes in their microstructure can mean big changes in the way they carry electricity.

The most commonly used semiconducting material is silicon. Like carbon, silicon atoms have four bonding electrons. Unlike carbon, the atoms of silicon do not form graphitelike crystal structures with one weakly bound electron per atom. Nor are the bonds in their crystal structures as powerful as the carbon bonds in diamonds. Electrons in silicon bonds can be shaken loose fairly easily by the normal vibration of the atoms. When that happens, they become conduction electrons.

For each conduction electron that shakes loose, a silicon atom is left with an empty bonding site. We call that empty site a "hole." As soon as the hole forms, the atom it leaves behind becomes a positively charged "ion" and that has powerful attraction for nearby electrons. Usually, one of the electrons from a neighboring atom falls into the hole soon after it forms. Thus a hole disappears from one atom and reappears "next door." It behaves as if it is a positive charge, moving from one spot to the next through the silicon.

Pure silicon always has an equal number of conduction electrons and holes. When it warms up, the atoms vibrate more; so at a higher temperature, it has more conduction electrons and holes. New pairs of conduction electrons and holes form constantly, but their number does not grow indefinitely. Sometimes a conduction electron falls into a hole and both disappear. That is called "annihilation." When the electron-hole annihilation rate matches the creation rate, the number of conduction electrons and holes remains steady.

These ultrapure cylinders of silicon are semiconductors ready to be transformed into thousands of computer chips. First they will be sliced into thin wafers. Then special machines put even thinner layers of other materials on the silicon or change its microstructure by carefully adding impurities, creating patterns for tens or hundreds of electronic chips on each wafer.

When people change the microstructure of semiconductors in small but carefully controlled ways, the movement of conduction electrons and holes—and therefore the conductivity—can change dramatically. For that reason, pure silicon turns out to be far less useful than "doped" silicon—silicon with small amounts of added impurities.

Let's examine what happens when we add a small amount of phosphorus or aluminum to a silicon crystal. A phosphorus atom has one more proton in its nucleus and one more electron than a silicon atom. The extra electron gives a phosphorus atom five bonding electrons. As an impurity in silicon, the phosphorus atom easily fits into a spot in the crystal arrangement, replacing a silicon atom. The replacement is not perfect, however, since only four of its five bonding electrons can find a place to connect. The fifth electron either becomes a conduction electron or fills a hole. Thus adding phosphorus creates a semiconducting material with an excess of conduction electrons and very few holes. We call that an "n-type" semiconductor because it has more negative than positive charges that are free to move.

Adding aluminum, which has one proton and one electron fewer than silicon, has the opposite effect. It also fits easily into the crystal arrangement, but with only three bonding electrons, its spot is one electron short. Soon a conduction electron comes along and is trapped, leaving a hole somewhere else with no electron to match it. The presence of aluminum atoms has created "p-type" silicon, a semiconducting material with positively charged holes but few conduction electrons.

SEMICONDUCTORS IN ELECTRONIC DEVICES

Semiconductors get down to business as Techno-Matter when people make them into electronic devices like diodes and transistors.

Diodes, One-way Electric Current Valves Putting a piece of p-type silicon next to a piece of n-type silicon creates a device that allows current to flow in one direction but not the opposite. Electronic engineers call that device a diode. The region where the two different types of material are joined is called a junction. Let's look at how it works.

Diagram A shows a battery with its positive terminal connected to the p-type portion of the diode and its negative terminal connected to the n-type. Since like charges repel, the positive terminal drives holes in the p-type semiconductor toward the junction. Likewise, the negative terminal drives conduction electrons in the n-type semiconductor toward the junction. There, the electrons and holes combine.

Meanwhile more conduction electrons flow from the negative terminal of the battery into the n-type material. Those replace the electrons that fell into holes at the junction. At the same time, the positive terminal of the battery attracts electrons from the p-type material. This creates holes to replace the ones filled by electrons at the junction. That means when the battery is connected as shown, electricity can flow steadily through the diode.

A diode is formed at the junction of an n-type region and a p-type region of a semiconductor. It permits electric current to flow only when a power source, such as a battery, is connected in the "forward biased" direction (diagram A), and blocks current from flowing in the "reverse biased" direction (diagram B).

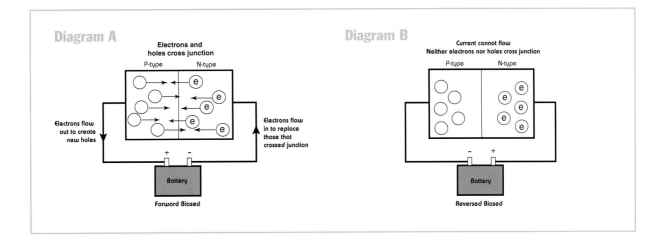

Diagram C

Operation of a Transistor

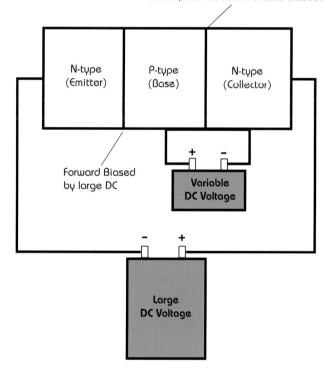

Reverse biased when variable voltage is low, but forward biased once variable voltage exceeds "threshold" value. Current flows when forward biased, but not when reverse biased.

N-type (Emitter)

P-type (Base)

N-type (Collector)

Forward Biased by large DC

+ −
Variable DC Voltage

− +

Large DC Voltage

A transistor is formed from two diodes back-to-back in an n-p-n or p-n-p sandwich.

Now suppose the battery terminals are connected in the opposite direction, as in diagram B. Since unlike charges attract, conduction electrons flow away from the junction and toward the positive battery terminal in the n-type material. Holes in the p-type region also move away from the junction. With neither electrons nor holes at the junction, current cannot flow across it.

Transistors, Electric Current Controllers A more complex arrangement of semiconducting materials is a device called a transistor. A common type of transistor resembles a sandwich with n-type material on the outside and p-type in the middle (or the other way around).

Diagram C shows the way an n-p-n transistor operates. A small change in voltage across the p-n junction produces a large change in the current through the whole device. Thus a transistor can be used as an amplifier—a device that produces large signals from small ones. Or it can be a controllable on-off switch, allowing or blocking the flow of current according to the "instruction" sent by a voltage signal across the p-n junction.

When used as a controllable switch, a transistor becomes the most important device in an electronic digital computer. Modern computers have millions or even billions of transistors, switching on and off millions of times in the blink of an eye. They are amazing devices, and the way people make and use them is the next chapter in the story of Techno-Matter.

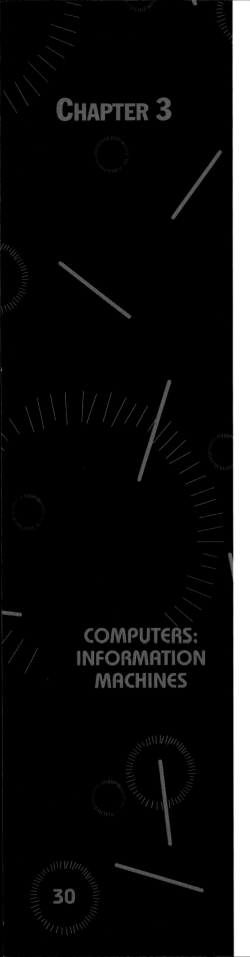

CHAPTER 3

DIGITAL MATTER

Computers, CD players, digital clocks, digital controls and displays, laser scanners and bar codes—everywhere you look or listen, you see or hear signs that we live in a digital world. Every week—or so it seems—a new machine or appliance with a microchip brain comes along to replace an old-fashioned one. The new device costs less than the old one did, and does more complicated tasks—better, in half the time, and often using half the energy.

How can that be? The answer is in the Techno-Matter that makes those wonderful digital devices possible.

When you think of the many ways people use computers, do you ever wonder about why we don't have another name for those versatile machines? Of course, people use computers for computation, or processing numbers, but they also use them to process many other kinds of information. For example, a computer can process text (letters and other symbols used for creating written documents), images, sound, or signals carried by electricity or radio waves.

No matter what kind of information the computer is processing, at the heart of its work lies computation. Every kind of information can be represented as numbers, just as if it is a secret code. A different number can stand for each letter of the alphabet or any other symbol used in writing. A document can be represented exactly and completely as a series of numbers.

A computer can divide an image into a series of picture elements, or "pixels." Each pixel can be represented by a two-number code, one to specify its color and the other its brightness. Sound can be transformed in a similar way. The ups and downs of air pressure can be turned into a series of numbers.

You usually think of numbers in the decimal system, which has ten different digits: 0, 1, 2, 3, 4, 5, 6, 7, 8, and 9. (Decimal comes from *deci-* the Latin root for ten.) For information machines, the binary system of two-different digits is more natural. *Bi-* comes from the Latin word for two, and the digits are 0 and 1.

You might tell your computer that humans first set foot on the Moon in 1969. Not to be outdone, a smart-aleck computer might reply that computers landed there three years earlier in the binary year 11,110,101,110.

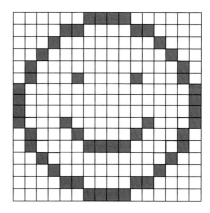

How do you spell "Have a nice day?"

3-192 12-48 16-8 32-4 64-2 68-34 128-1 128-1 128-1 136-17 68-34 67-194 32-4 16-8 12-48 3-192

Turn these sixteen pairs of numbers into pairs of eight-bit binary numbers. Then represent "0" as a light square and "1" as a dark square. Arrange the pairs as sixteen small squares across each of sixteen rows from top to bottom. The result is this familiar pattern.

Why is the binary system so natural for computers? Because computers use on-off switches instead of symbols. They use the off position to represent "0" and the on position to represent "1." Perhaps that gives you an idea why semiconductors like silicon are so important for computing. If you want to turn a signal into a number, you'd look for a device that uses

ELECTRONIC DIGITAL MATTER

You are used to representing numbers in the decimal system. Suppose you weigh 87 pounds. How do you interpret "87"? You go from right to left. In the right-most, or "ones," column is the symbol "7," and in the next column to the left, or "tens," column is the symbol "8." The value of 87 is 7 + 8x10. Each column farther to the left has ten times the basic value of the preceding one. The column can contain any of ten different digits from zero through nine.

In the binary system, each column further to the left has two times the value of the preceding one. The columns are the ones, twos, fours, eights, and so on. Each column contains one of only two digits, zero or one. An 87-pound person's weight is 1010111 in the binary system (1 + 1x2 + 1x4 + 0x8 + 1x16 + 0x32 + 1x64 or 1 + 2 + 4 + 16 + 64 = 87). Binary digits are called **bits** for short.

that signal to turn a set of switches on or off, creating the number in binary code. A transistor is perfect for the task.

Before transistors were invented, computers were large, cumbersome, and not very common. They were usually room-size devices with thousands of vacuum tubes, and they were used mainly for long, complicated calculations. They required large amounts of electricity and produced lots of heat, but they could carry out computations that had only been dreamed of up to that time.

When transistors came along, the age of semiconductor electronics began. Computers were still large, but they were becoming more common and more powerful. The first transistors were about the size of a housefly and used much less electric current than vacuum tubes. They also worked faster, because their signals traveled shorter distances. Best of all, they could do more because engineers could now build more complex circuits. Soon businesses used computers for both computation and record keeping, and everyday people realized that computers were changing their lives.

Probably the greatest breakthrough in computing came with the invention of the integrated circuit. Instead of adding impurities to silicon to make a single transistor, manufacturers learned how to create several transistors and their interconnecting wires on a small semiconducting chip.

Soon, the number of transistors on a chip grew into the thousands. The first important integrated circuits gave computers large, fast memories. Each memory chip contained thousands of microscopic on-off switches, just what computers need to store binary information. The chips also had microscopic aluminum pathways. Those were the wires used to carry signals within the memory and out to the rest of the computer.

Computers have come a long way since those first memory chips. Now memory chips contain not thousands but millions of switches. Other more complicated chips, called microprocessors, carry out the main computation tasks. A modern microprocessor chip can do everything that the early room-size computers did, using a tiny fraction of the energy in a tiny fraction of the time for a tiny fraction of the cost. Because of microprocessors, stores have computers in every cash register, businesses have computers on many desks, and many families have computers in their homes.

A vacuum tube and an early transistor that replaced it

VACUUM TUBES ARE BETTER THAN NOTHING

You may be wondering about vacuum tubes. A vacuum, after all, is a space that contains nothing. Vacuum tubes are no longer very common, but they once were at the heart of all kinds of electronic devices, like radios, televisions, and computers. They were small glass bulbs, shaped something like an upright cylinder with a round cap on top. Most would fit comfortably in your hand. The glass was clear and thicker than a lightbulb. The bases of the tubes were made of hard insulating materials.

Inside the tubes were special pieces of metal. Some were filaments, like the glowing parts of electric lightbulbs. Those released electrons when they got very hot. Others were screens or metal sheets. Small metal pins connected to those pieces passed through the base of the tube to the outside. Before the tubes were sealed to their bases, the air was pumped out. Like the semiconducting diodes and transistors that replaced them, vacuum tubes could act as one-way valves for electric current, amplifiers, or controllable switches. Each type of vacuum tube was precisely designed; the shape and spacing of those metal parts, and the connections between them, produced the exact electronic behavior needed.

If you look at a magnified picture of an integrated circuit, you can see several different regions, and each one has its own pattern of lines. To create those chips and patterns, engineers go through many steps. The process is called "microfabrication," because the smallest features on the chips are about a micrometer—a millionth of a meter—in size.

Before they can create the integrated circuit, the engineers first melt and purify silicon. As it cools and solidifies, the silicon is drawn into a large cylinder with a nearly perfect crystal structure. The engineers then slice that cylinder into thin wafers. Each wafer will eventually become hundreds of chips.

The picture shows a wafer with a pattern of rectangles on it. By the time the chip making is finished, each of those rectangles will be transformed into an integrated circuit. The chips are built up layer by layer, like precisely baked cakes, using a process quite similar to photography.

When chip makers create a layer, their first step is to apply a light-sensitive coating to the wafer. Next, they shine light onto the coating through a patterned mask. The light causes a chemical change in the exposed region, just as it does in photographic film. In the next step, they apply a chemical developer to dissolve away the unexposed material. That leaves the exposed material behind as a negative. At that point, they add a new material where the unexposed coating used to be. That material—in the pattern of the original mask—might be n-type or p-type silicon to create parts of the transistors; it might be metal to create tiny wires; or it might be an insulating material. Finally the exposed coating is removed and the layer is finished.

Then the process of making the next layer begins. This continues through several layers until the chip is finally finished. The icing is on the cake at last! If you think that sounds difficult and expensive, you're right and you're wrong. It is difficult, and it does cost a lot of money to make a wafer. But a single wafer can contain hundreds of chips, and a single chip can contain thousands or even millions of transistors. When you figure out the cost **per transistor**, it is amazingly inexpensive.

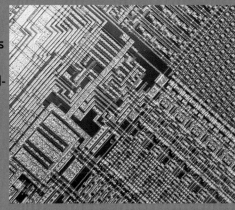

This magnified picture of an integrated circuit shows many different microfabricated regions. This entire section is about 0.7 millimeters wide and 0.6 millimeters high, so small that about 400 pieces that size could be lined up 20 by 20 on an average adult thumbnail.

Electronic digital matter is only part of the story. Magnetic digital Techno-Matter, though less well known, is equally fascinating.

Semiconductor memory chips in a computer are mostly the kind known as "random access memory," or RAM. When a computer program calls for information to be written into or read from RAM, the computer can quickly find (access) the location of that information in whatever order the program specifies—even if it is a random sequence.

You might think RAM is all the memory a computer might need, but RAM chips have two major drawbacks. First, they lose their information when the power goes off. Second, although the cost of one bit is low and getting lower, the number of bits computers need keeps growing and growing. Advanced computers and programs need millions or billions of bits of memory.

Is there a less expensive type of Techno-Matter with the special—almost magical—properties computer memories need? The answer is yes, magnetic materials. Once again the magic is in the microstructure.

You have certainly seen permanent magnets in your home, and you have probably experimented with them. You know that a magnet has two opposite ends, called poles. Just as with positive and negative electric charges, opposite poles attract and like poles repel. We could call them positive and negative poles; but we call them north and south instead, because the Earth itself is a magnet. If you hang a magnet on a string, its north pole points approximately northward because of the influence of the planetary magnet.

Magnetism and electricity are closely related; they are two sides of the same basic force called electromagnetism. You probably know that an electric current in a coil of wire acts like a magnet. You can magnetize a sewing needle by putting

Computer hard disks and heads are made of specially engineered materials. The disks have many layers, including a thin layer of magnetic material called the recording medium. The head is an almost invisible electromagnet, microfabricated onto a tiny chip of silicon. As the disk spins, the head skims just above the surface like a tiny airplane on a cushion of air much thinner than a human hair.

it in the middle of the coil, and you can reverse its poles by putting it in the opposite way. That is the principle behind magnetic information storage. Imagine a line of magnetized needles, end to end. If the magnetic direction changes, it represents a binary digit of "1"; if the magnetic direction does not change, that bit is a "0."

An electromagnet can create or "write" a magnetic pattern of bits, but how can you read it? The answer is that moving a coil of wire past a magnet—or the magnet past the coil—can cause an electric current to flow. That is the way electric generators work. When a coil moves past a region with a changing magnetic direction, a little pulse of current flows. That means the bit is a "1." No change in magnetic direction means no current, so the bit is a "0."

Magnetic information can be recorded on a magnetic material called a medium (plural, media), and written or read by a coil of wire called a head. The least expensive medium is magnetic tape, similar to what you find in sound or video recorders. The problem with tapes is the long time it takes to get to the spot where the computer will read or write information. It's not good for random access, because you might have to move from one end of the tape to the other, again and again, to get the information you need.

Magnetic diskettes use a similar medium and a similar head. They don't need as much time to get to the right place to read or write information, but it still takes a while since the diskette may have to spin a full turn. Getting to the right place is not the only problem. With RAM, information can be moved very quickly. Magnetic memories are much slower. If you need to move more quickly from one bit to the next, then the bits must either be made smaller or the motion must be speedier.

That's where "hard disks" come in. They're still much slower than RAM, but their bits are very close together and they spin at high speed. Hard-disk drives aren't fast enough for random access, but they don't cause great delays when a computer program instruction says to write information on them or read information from them.

Materials scientists and engineers have worked hard to make special magnetic media for hard disks. Their microstructure allows them to have a magnetic pattern with very tiny bits very close together. To read and write those bits, the heads not only have to be minuscule themselves, but they must also get very close to the media. As the disks turn, the heads fly over the media like tiny airplanes, so close that there is no room for the tiniest bump or speck of dust.

To protect the magnetic media from "head crashes," engineers coat them with very thin layers of a very smooth, hard material. To make heads so small, engineers built them layer by layer on silicon wafers, as if they were making integrated circuits.

That's only the beginning of the story. We could fill this book with facts, figures, and details about hard-disk drives—about the many layers of carefully designed materials in the media and the microstructures that make them work, and about the equally astounding heads and their microstructures. Every year brings new surprises in Techno-Matter. Every year, heads and magnetic bits get smaller, hard-disk drives get faster, and the computers that use them become more powerful and useful in many more ways.

THE POWER OF DIGITAL DEVICES

Computers are now in places you might never imagine: in home appliances, radios, televisions, VCRs, and CD players; in telephones and wristwatches; under the hoods of cars.

Computers are doing all kinds of things in all kinds of places. Yet we are really just beginning. Computers will be getting smaller, faster, cheaper, and more powerful for years to come. People will be making chips with more and tinier transistors on chips. Magnetic information storage devices will hold more information in less space, will write and read it faster, and will probably cost less than the remarkable disk drives of today.

Yet that is only the beginning. Someday, digital devices that rely on electronic and magnetic properties of matter may be as outdated as vacuum tubes. Future computers may be built from new forms of Techno-Matter that use light or even atoms to store and process binary information. Looking back to the time before computers, we can see that we have traveled a long way; but the years ahead promise even more astonishing advances to come—thanks in great part to the work of materials scientists and materials engineers.

POLY-MATTER

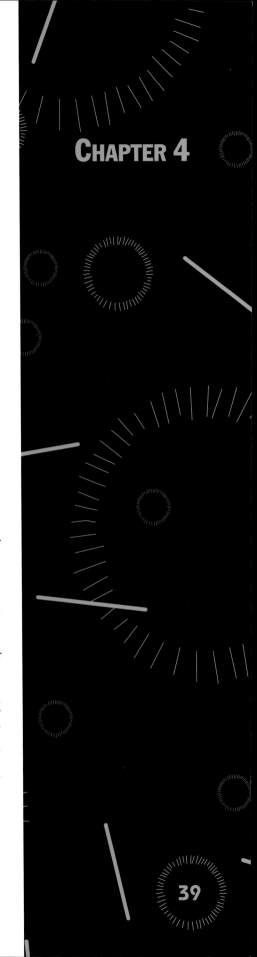

One of the most famous scenes in the history of American movies is in the 1967 film *The Graduate*. A successful executive calls aside a young man who has just graduated from college and offers him a one-word secret of success: "Plastics!"

The executive's advice was good then, and it is good now; but this chapter advises you to go one step further: "Polymers!"

Plastics are just one example of a much larger class of materials. You know polymers in many forms besides plastics: synthetic fabrics, nonstick coatings, adhesives, and different kinds of rubber, to name a few. Polymers also have many other uses, for example as lubricants or surfactants (molecules that attach themselves to and change the properties of the surface of a substance).

The word "polymer" comes from the Greek *poly*, meaning many, and *meros*, meaning part. The name describes the nature of the polymer molecule, which is, in fact, made up mainly of many repeating units, or "mers," combined together. A single polymer molecule can have hundreds or thousands of repetitions of its basic unit. Because it is so long, scientists often use the term "macromolecule" (from the Greek *makros*, meaning long) to describe it.

The properties of polymers, like all other materials, depend on their microstructure. In the case of polymers, much of the microstructure is in the makeup of the macromolecule itself. That microstructure is determined by not only the number of units and the atoms in those units but also by the shape of the molecules. There can be substantial differences in microstructure—and thus in properties— between molecules that are part of the same polymer family.

Macromolecules and the products made from them take many different forms. Polymers are found in so many places and have so many uses in modern technology that this chapter is only a small peek at a large and fascinating subject.

THE CHEMISTRY OF CARBON

Nearly all of today's polymers are based on the chemistry of carbon. A few, such as silicones and polysilanes, are based on silicon, but we will focus on carbon-based polymers. As you discovered in Chapter 1, each carbon can form up to four bonds with other atoms. In Chapter 2, you discovered that the bonds come from sharing electrons between atoms. In graphite for example, three of the bonds attach one carbon atom to other carbon atoms in a "chicken-wire" arrangement.

In polymer molecules, carbon atoms often bond to each other in chains or rings. Sometimes the bonds between two carbon atoms involve two or three shared electrons per atom instead of one. These double and triple bonds leave fewer bonding electrons available for combining with other atoms.

A simple introduction to the chemistry of carbon is the class of compounds called hydrocarbons, which contain only hydrogen and carbon. Let's start with the so-called saturated hydrocarbons, which have the maximum possible number of hydrogen atoms because all the carbon atoms form single bonds. The simplest of these is methane, with the chemical formula CH_4. Then comes ethane, C_2H_6, propane, C_3H_8, and so on. Formulas like those tell how many of each type of atom a molecule has but do not show the bonds between the atoms. For that, chemists use structural formulas like these:

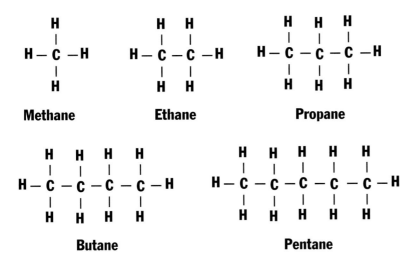

In the structural formulas, bonds are shown by lines between atoms. Double bonds are shown by a double line and triple bonds are shown by a triple line. For example, look at the structural formulas for the "unsaturated" hydrocarbons ethylene, C_2H_4, and ethyne (or acetylene), C_2H_2. They are called unsaturated because the hydrocarbon could add more hydrogen by replacing double bonds with single ones (or triple bonds with either double or single ones).

Often, the same chemical formula can result from two different structures, as for octane and *n*-octane, C_8H_{18}, as shown here:

These are ball-and-stick molecular models of hydrocarbons octane and *n*-octane, chemical formula C_8H_{18}. The atoms are spherical and color-coded: the carbon atoms are darker and hydrogen atoms lighter in both models. The *n* refers to the straight chain form, in which all the carbons are arranged in an unbranched line, as seen here. Octane (right) is the more complicated of the two, having a branched structure. Octane and *n*-octane are distilled from crude oil largely for use in gasoline.

N-Octane

Octane

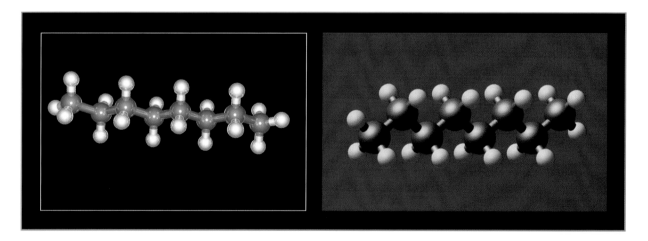

Notice that the carbons in the n-octane molecule make a straight line, while the carbons in the octane branch off the main chain. Thus n-octane is said to be a linear molecule, while octane is called branched. In fact, you could describe this form of octane as pentane that has had three of its hydrogens replaced by CH_3 (methyl) groups. Replacing one atom or group with another atom or group is a common way to make new carbon compounds. As you can imagine, chemists can use that approach to make larger and larger molecules—and to make an enormous variety of them.

When chemists do that, they are following a process that happened quite naturally in the development of living things. Thus they often call the branch of chemistry dealing with the many varieties of carbon compounds "organic." Many compounds in naturally occurring organic materials, such as wood, rubber, and animal skin, are polymers.

Even deoxyribonucleic acid—the famous DNA that is the basis of life—is a polymer that contains two long coils of atoms linked by a series of units of four basic types. The order in which those units occurs determines whether the life-form is a fungus, a plant, an animal, or a human. If it is a human or animal, the DNA determines its sex, the color of its skin, hair, and eyes, and many other things about it. Unless you have an identical twin, your DNA is slightly different from everyone else's in the world.

With all that variety possible in the chemistry of carbon, it is no wonder that materials scientists and engineers have worked so hard to understand the properties of polymers and to create new ones. Let's examine some of the things that they have learned and what they can do with their knowledge.

LINEAR POLYMERS

Suppose you were to take an atom of ethylene (C_2H_4) and partially break the double bond between its two carbon atoms, leaving a single bond and two unbonded—or "free"—electrons. You can view those free electrons as partial bonds, ready to join with other free electrons, so the structural formula might look like this:

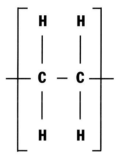

Ethylene mer

If two of these units were to come together, they would join, forming a chain of four carbon atoms attached to eight hydrogen atoms with free electrons at both ends. Other units could attach onto those ends, and the chain would continue to grow, and grow, andgrowandgrowandgrowandgrow. The very large chain eventually will stop growing when the free electrons at the ends join with something that has no free electrons of its own, but by then a macromolecule of polyethylene has been created.

Polyethylene is a very common plastic material. It is the simplest of the linear polymers, that is those polymers with long chain molecules. Other well-known linear polymers are the vinyl family, in which one of the hydrogens of the ethylene mer is replaced by a different atom or group. For example, the unit of polyvinyl chloride is simply ethylene with a chlorine atom (Cl) in place of one of its hydrogen atoms, like this:

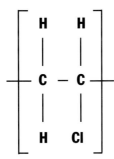

Vinyl chloride mer

Polystyrene is another member of the vinyl family. You probably know it best as Styrofoam. Styrofoam is made by blowing a gas through polystyrene as it forms. You probably know it from beverage cups at fast-food restaurants or packing "peanuts" that keep fragile items from breaking when they are shipped.

Styrene, the basic unit of polystyrene, contains a group of six carbon atoms arranged in a closed loop with alternating single and double bonds. That arrangement is called a benzene ring after the hydrocarbon benzene, C_6H_6, that has that structure. In polystyrene, the basic unit is formed by replacing one of the six hydrogen atoms of a benzene ring with an ethylene mer.

One of the most famous polymers is the linear macromolecule polytetrafluoroethylene, better known as Teflon. If you analyze its name, you may be able to figure out that all four of the hydrogen atoms of ethylene are replaced by fluorine (F) atoms, so its unit looks like this:

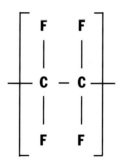

Tetrafluoroethylene mer

Other well-known classes of linear polymers are the polyesters, useful in fiber form for clothing, and polyurethanes, which form useful foams. Natural rubber is a linear polymer that forms inside plants. Materials scientists have learned to tailor the properties of these substances by varying the lengths of the molecules' chains and the microstructure that results when many long-chain molecules get together.

MAKING POLYMERS

Some polymers, like polyethylene, are made by addition of molecules with nothing left over. In order to make that happen, chemists have to do something to break a double bond and create the free electrons that start the polymerization process.

Other polymers form when atoms or groups of atoms at opposite ends of a molecule combine to form a small molecule, like water. The remaining material can then chain together, leaving the water behind. The best-known example of this is the molecule shown directly below.

When this molecule chains together, the hydrogen and hydroxyl at the ends form water and leave behind the well-known polymer nylon.

It is based on pentane, a five-carbon saturated hydrocarbon. At the left end, a common chemical group known as "amine" with the formula NH_2 (N is the symbol for a nitrogen atom) replaces a hydrogen atom. Replacing the hydrogen at the right end is a COOH group. O is the symbol for oxygen, OH is a bonded hydrogen-oxygen unit known as hydroxide or a hydroxyl group, and the COOH combination is part of every alcohol molecule.

Under proper conditions, a hydrogen atom from the amine group of one atom will combine with the hydroxyl group of another, forming a molecule of water. That leaves behind a chain of two units, again with a hydrogen at one end and a hydroxyl on the other. The reaction can continue, producing larger chains and more water molecules.

The polymer product produced in this reaction is nylon, a strong, shiny fiber that revolutionized the way people dressed. Before 1938, silk stockings and shirts were the symbol of wealth and elegance; afterward, almost everyone could afford clothes that looked smooth and shiny.

The new fabric became so popular that women called their stockings "nylons," but that was not all nylon was good for. Nylon cords were so strong and durable that they were used in automobile tires, among other things.

POLYMER MICROSTRUCTURE

Many of the unusual properties of polymeric materials can be understood by thinking about the unusual microstructures that their large molecules can lead to. Linear polymer molecules look and behave much like a chain of beads. If the chain is long enough, or if many chains come together, the molecule can organize itself into patterns.

The chains can be stiff or flexible, straight or kinky. Rubber molecules are very kinky chains, which gives rubber its stretchability. When you pull on a piece of rubber, you straighten the kinks of its molecules!

Natural rubber is so stretchable that it is gooey. Before it can be used in tires, it needs to be stiffer and bouncier. You may have heard the story of how Charles Goodyear discovered, quite by accident, that adding some sulfur to rubber makes it stiffer and bouncier without losing its flexibility. He called his product "vulcanized" rubber and went on to make a fortune in the tire business.

Today we understand that the stiffness of vulcanized rubber comes from chemical links that the sulfur forms between different parts of a linear molecule. Think of a chain of a thousand beads that has arranged itself into a snakelike S shape. Perhaps the 57th bead on one arm of the S is in contact with the 288th bead on a different arm, and many other pairs of beads are in similar contact.

By pulling on the ends of the chain, it would be easy to break those connections. The chain could easily be stretched to many times its length, and it would be slow to return to its old shape. When it does return, bead number 57 may now be in contact with bead number 240.

But now suppose you were to put springs between some of those beads on different parts of the S. That would make the connections permanent and the chain would return to its old shape more quickly. That's the way vulcanizing works. By adding chemical connections between mers that happen to be near each other, sulfur gives natural rubber the springiness it needs to be used in tires.

Chemists call that process "cross-linking." Cross-linking turns one-dimensional chains into three-dimensional structures that can make a polymer very hard. It is also the process that makes superadhesives work; they form a joint that is often stronger than the materials they are connecting by a chemical reaction that creates a tangle of cross-links.

This chapter is only the beginning of the story of polymers. If we tried to tell the rest of the story, we wouldn't have room for all the other kinds of Techno-Matter.

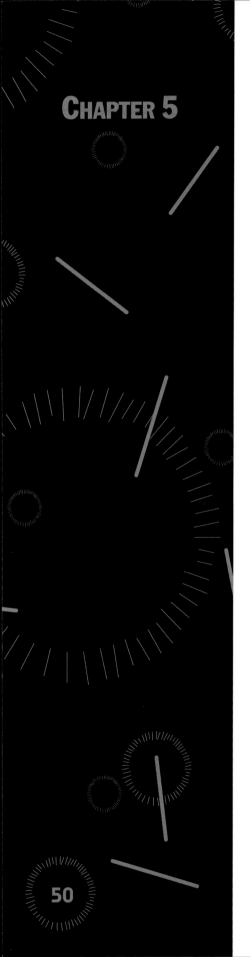

CHAPTER 5

OLD-NEW MATTER

The story of Techno-Matter is the story of human progress. By using the newest human-made materials, we create amazing machines and devices to improve our lives. Yet the modern fields of materials science and engineering have ancient roots.

You may think that the creation of new materials sets us apart from people of earlier times. But that isn't really so. From before the dawn of recorded history, people have not only been making tools and machines—things we call "technology"—but they have also been discovering new materials. Just as happens today, the new technologies of those times would never have come into being without new materials. So before we take a closer look at today's materials, let's go back to when technology started, more than two million years ago in a period we now call the Stone Age.

By today's standards, Stone Age technology is not very impressive. But two million years ago, humans discovered that hitting stones together can make them into sharp tools and weapons. That led to enormous changes. No longer did people simply try to survive in their environment; rather, they actively looked for ways to change the environment to their advantage.

Still, Stone Age people had to rely on the materials that nature gave them: animal skins, bones, teeth, and sinews, fibers from plants, wood from trees, earth, and of course, rocks and stones. That situation changed about ten thousand years ago when people discovered that they could make their own stone-like material by heating clay in a fire. Today, we would call that first human-made material a ceramic. Whatever those early people called it, they knew that they could form it into pots, bowls, jugs, and many other kinds of useful objects. This was the first new technology based on a material not found in nature, and it changed the way people lived.

Pottery must have seemed like amazing techno-matter to the Stone Age people who discovered that heating clay could transform it into what to them was an entirely new substance.

About three thousand years after that, people discovered how to use metals. Metallurgy began with people's fascination with nuggets of copper and gold that they found in the ground. Then came the discovery that metals did not chip like stone but rather could be pounded into useful shapes.

Other important discoveries followed. People learned how to melt metals and make objects of various shapes by pouring the molten metal into a mold. This process, called casting, could create metal tools and weapons in shapes that could not be made with stone. But since metal was rare and metal tools wore out more easily than those made of stone, people continued to use stone tools more than metal ones. That began to change with the discovery of two important metallurgical processes: smelting and alloying.

In smelting, a substance called an ore is heated in a furnace, sometimes with another substance, producing a metal. Ores are much more common than pure metals, so the discovery of smelting greatly increased the amount of metal in the world. In alloying, two or more different metals are mixed together, usually in the molten state. The resulting material, called an alloy, is often more useful than the metals that went into it.

Besides increasing the amount of metal, smelting also led to the discovery of new metals, such as tin. Tin, by itself, did not seem to be very useful, but because its ore was found with copper ore, people naturally tried mixing it with copper. The result was a very useful alloy called bronze, first discovered about 5,500 years ago.

Bronze turned out to be the Techno-Matter of the Stone Age. It was as strong as stone and could be cast into many useful shapes. Because bronze tools had better shapes than stone tools and were just as strong and easier to make, stone tools were suddenly obsolete. With the creation of another material not found in nature, civilization changed dramatically. The Stone Age had ended and the Bronze Age had begun.

During the Bronze Age, people made many useful discoveries about metals and alloys. For example, people discovered that bronze became stronger when they beat it while it was hot. They also continued to discover new ores and new metals. Despite the discoveries, people found nothing to equal bronze for a long time. Finally, around 1900 B.C., another metallurgical breakthrough occurred: People discovered how to smelt iron from its ore, a very common mineral that we now know is a form of iron oxide.

Iron was already known because it is the main component of some meteorites, but it was very rare. After the discovery of how to smelt it, iron became very important because it became far more plentiful than bronze, and it was nearly as useful. People who knew how to smelt iron were able to make many more metal objects than before. Over the next seven centuries, as the new knowledge spread, civilization underwent a slow and gradual change from the Bronze Age to the Iron Age.

Iron became even more important following the accidental discovery that reheating it in a charcoal fire after smelting made it stronger. The result was an iron-carbon alloy that we now know as steel. As centuries passed, steelmaking gradually improved; people learned how to make more steel and how to make it better. By the middle of the eighteenth century, people knew how to make large quantities of high-strength, high-quality steel. That knowledge, together with the invention of the steam engine, transformed the Iron Age into the Industrial Revolution.

Discovering how to change iron into steel by heating it with carbon was a major impetus of the Industrial Revolution.

During the Bronze Age, people also discovered how to turn sand into glass, another very useful material. Like ceramics and metals, glass has played an important role in human technology for many centuries.

So looking back on civilization from the Stone Age to the Bronze Age to the Iron Age to the Industrial Revolution of steam and steel, we see again and again the technological importance of the discovery of new materials.

Today, we are in the midst of a period of change more dramatic than ever, a period driven by an explosion of new technology and new materials. What kinds of materials are

those, you may ask. The answer is surprising. Many of today's greatest advances in materials science and engineering have been made in the oldest of human-made materials: metals, ceramics, and glass.

What makes these materials so promising? As you have come to expect, the answer is the microstructure. Although this book does not have room to give all the details, it's worth setting a few pages aside to describe what science and engineering can do with the microstructure of each of these old-new materials.

Although smelting, alloying, and forming metals are among our oldest technologies, the science and engineering of metallurgy are relatively new. People are continuing to learn more about metals and to find new ways to use them.

Strength and malleability (the ease of changing shape) are still major reasons people use metals, but other properties are also important. Some metals, like aluminum and magnesium, are useful because they are relatively light. Others, like lead, tungsten, and uranium, are useful because they are heavy. Tungsten is also useful because it gets hot enough to glow brightly without melting, while lead-containing alloys like solder and Wood's metal (used in sprinkler systems) are useful because they melt at relatively low temperatures. There are metals like copper, silver, and gold that people use when they need a good conductor of heat or electricity. But when people make a heating element, they need a not-so-good electrical conductor that can get very hot without melting, like the alloy called nichrome. If they need something powerfully magnetic, there are alloys that are far more magnetic than iron. If they need something nonmagnetic, there are many metals and alloys to fill the bill.

As that list of properties tells you, metals and alloys have many uses. The object of the science of metallurgy is to understand the microstructure of metals and alloys and to learn how to change it. Metallurgical engineers use that scientific knowledge to create metallic Techno-Matter.

Single-Phase and Multiphase Metals To begin to understand the properties of metals and alloys, we start with their crystal structure. Although people usually think of crystals as perfect arrangements of atoms or molecules, many of the important properties of real crystalline materials are determined by imperfections or impurities, such as in semiconductors used as diodes or transistors. That is certainly true of metals and alloys. Looking closely at the microstructure of a metal or alloy, you may discover that it is not a single material at all.

If you examine the microstructure of a metal or alloy, you will discover that it has many small regions, called grains, with nearly perfect crystal structures. If the microstructure of the grains is similar throughout the metal or alloy, we call it single-phase. If the microstructure is different from one grain to the next, we call it multiphase.

Bronze, which was the first alloy discovered by humans, is a single-phase metal. Its important properties come from imperfections in the crystal structure in those grains. Steel is very different. Its important properties come from its multiphase alloy structure.

Many details of microstructure influence the properties of single-phase metals. One of the most important is the size of its grains. Each grain is really a separate crystal within the metal. Small grains give the metal greater resistance to wear. It's hard to get a good grip on something so tiny and wedged in so tightly among other grains. Small grains also reduce its conductivity of heat and electricity. Heat and electrical energy flow easily within a grain, but the grain boundaries are obstacles to that flow.

Grain size is also a very important factor in the properties of multiphase metals, especially since neighboring grains may have different compositions or crystal structures from each other.

Iron and Steel Without question, steel is the most widely used, versatile, and important metal product in the history of human civilization. Its major component is iron, the second most common metal in the earth's crust, and one that is easily extracted from its ore by smelting. (Aluminum, the most common metal, requires enormous amounts of electrical energy to free it from its ore. Furthermore, most aluminum occurs in clays, which are not suitable as ore.)

The term "steel" actually includes a large family of iron-based alloys. Besides iron, steel contains about 0.5 percent carbon (sometimes more but always less than 1.2 percent). By adding varying amounts of other elements (up to 5 percent), steelmakers produce a huge variety of products.

Steel is a complex multiphase material. Its strength comes from grains of iron carbide, which is a ceramic material also called cementite. (Ceramics, as you will read in the next section, are usually very hard, but very brittle materials.) Because the brittle cementite is surrounded by iron, the steel retains iron's ability to be shaped while gaining toughness from the hard ceramic grains.

This micrograph of iron is magnified 1,000 times. It shows ceramic nodules and bits of carbon.

Simply by changing the carbon content, it is possible to produce a wide range of microstructures and properties of steel. And that is only the beginning. You would have to read a more advanced book than this to learn about what happens when you add different elements to the mix or when you process the steel in different ways. That book might also tell you about many other important metals and alloys. It would surely contain details of the following important processes in metallurgy.

• **Smelting** As you already read, metallurgy begins with smelting, the process of extracting a metal from its ore using heat.

• **Electrolysis** Running an electric current through a chemical compound can reverse the chemical reaction that formed it. That is another way of extracting a metal from its ore, but it requires an enormous amount of electrical energy. Electrolysis is only used when ordinary smelting will not work. The only metal produced in large quantities in this way is aluminum.

• **Alloying and Quenching** Two or more metals may be melted and mixed together to form alloys. The molten mixture may be cooled slowly, or it may be cooled very quickly in a process called quenching. Different cooling rates produce very different microstructures and properties.

• **Cold- and Hot-Working** One of the most important discoveries of the Bronze Age was the strengthening of metals by beating them, especially when they are hot. We now know that such changes are due to the motion of crystal defects, which changes the microstructure.

• **Annealing** The process of annealing involves heating a material to near its melting point and then letting it remain there for an extended time. That allows atoms, molecules, or crystal defects to move from place to place, leading to significant changes in microstructure. One frequent result of annealing is grain growth.

The effects on the properties of metals from annealing, quenching, and cold- and hot-working have been known for many centuries; but only recently have we come to understand their effects on microstructure. With that understanding, we can now create new metallic materials with made-to-order electrical, magnetic, and other properties.

CERAMICS AND GLASS

The Stone Age makes up the first 99.7 percent of the two-million-year history of human civilization. Putting that history on a time scale comparable to your own life, the Stone Age ended about two weeks ago. So although you may think of it as ancient history, you should also realize that the Stone Age shaped human behavior in many ways that continue today.

It is somewhat deceptive to say that the Stone Age ended when the Bronze Age began. Bronze made great tools and weapons in many ways, but stone and ceramic items still had many significant advantages, and they were made from the most common natural materials. So although bronze revolutionized civilization, stone and ceramic items continued to be very important.

Bronze and other alloys did not replace ceramics; rather, they supplemented them. In fact, although the new materials got most of the attention, people continued to work with the old ones, finding new and better ways to make and use them.

With every new "Age," the materials of the previous period of history continue to be valuable. And, in every age, some of the biggest breakthroughs come from the oldest materials. That is certainly true of ceramics and glasses. So as the twenty-first century begins, it is fair to say that the Stone Age continues.

The Chemistry and Microstructure of Ceramics and Glass Ceramics and glass are different forms of the same chemical substances. Ceramics are crystalline, while glass is "amorphous." Amorphous, which means without form, describes an arrangement of atoms and molecules in an irregular pattern, as if they are in a liquid, although the substance is solid (that is, its atoms or molecules do not move past one another). For that reason some people consider glass a "super-cooled liquid" instead of an amorphous solid.

Ceramic substances are chemical compounds of metals (or semimetals like silicon or carbon) and nonmetals, bound together by powerful chemical bonds. The bonds get their strength from the fact that they usually involve two or more electrons from each atom or group of atoms.

Aluminum oxide (two aluminum atoms bound to three oxygens) and silicon dioxide (one silicon atom bound to two oxygens) are both ceramic materials. In fact, most ceramics are oxides or silicates (compounds containing the silicate group—a common chemical unit made of one silicon atom plus three oxygen atoms). This should not be surprising, since oxygen and silicon are the two most common atoms in the Earth's crust (47% and 28% respectively, by weight).

Aluminum is also common in ceramics because it is the third most prevalent atom in the Earth's crust (although, by weight, there is less aluminum than iron). The rocks of the earth are natural ceramics (or glass, in the case of volcanic rocks like obsidian).

The strong bonds are responsible for ceramic materials' most useful properties. For example, ceramics can withstand high pressures because the bonds make it difficult to change the distances between atoms. Also ceramics can withstand very high temperatures without melting because it takes more thermal energy before the atoms vibrate enough to disrupt the crystal structure. Finally ceramics (and glass) are highly resistant to corrosion. That is because corrosion is a chemical reaction in which metallic atoms or ions gain electrons, but in ceramics, the metal atoms have already gained electrons as part of those bonds.

Another characteristic property of ceramics is their brittleness. They are so hard that they will break along a crack rather than stretch or bend when pulled or twisted. The breaks follow grain boundaries or other crystal defects.

Applications of Ceramics The hardness, heat resistance, and corrosion resistance of ceramics clearly make them attractive materials. But what about the brittleness? For us, brittleness can be a disadvantage, but for early humans, who had only the ceramics that nature provided—rocks and stones—brittleness was an asset. It enabled them to break off pieces of the stones to make sharp-edged tools.

Today, most ceramics in use are not natural stone. Rather, like all other modern materials, they are made in ways that control their microstructure to enhance desirable properties and minimize undesirable ones. Here are a few of the important applications of ceramics.

The tiles that protect the United States space shuttles from the heat of reentry are made of a specially developed refractory ceramic material. Previously, when space vehicles were not reusable, heat protection was provided by a material that flaked off when it got hot, carrying the heat away. Current space shuttle tiles can provide protection from temperatures that can reach 2300°F, but 3500°F reentry temperatures will not be unusual for future astronauts venturing beyond Earth orbit.

• Refractory Materials Materials that can withstand very high temperatures are called "refractory." Refractory materials are most commonly used as linings for furnaces, so they must have not only high melting points but also have low thermal conductivity and maintain their strength at high temperatures.

The tiles that protect the United States space shuttles from the heat of reentry are made of a specially developed refractory ceramic material. Previously, when space vehicles were not reusable, heat protection was provided by a material that flaked off as it got hot, carrying the heat away. The space shuttle tiles provide permanent protection.

• Abrasives Grinding and cutting are common industrial processes. Ceramics, because of their hardness, are commonly used on grinding wheels and cutting tools. Natural

and synthetic (manufactured) gemstones, and human-made ceramics like the carbides of boron, silicon, titanium, and tungsten are important abrasive materials.

• **Insulators** Ceramics are excellent electrical insulators because the bonds between the atoms tie up the conduction electrons quite effectively. Power lines are usually protected by insulators made of electrical porcelain, a ceramic not very different from that used for plumbing fixtures. Not only does that ceramic have exceptionally high electrical resistance, it can also withstand a high voltage without "breakdown" (a sudden surge of electricity through a material in much the way lightning flashes through the air when the voltage between two nearby clouds is high enough).

• **Piezoelectrics** Some ceramics exhibit a property called piezoelectricity, which gets its name from the Greek word *piezein*, meaning push. A piezoelectric material produces an electric current or voltage when the pressure on it changes. In a piezoelectric crystal, the positive and negative ions in the substance tend to be on opposite sides of each lattice site. When you change the pressure, the oppositely charged ions move a little closer together or farther apart, so there is a pulse of electric current.

Piezoelectric crystals have many uses as pressure sensors. They are also used as vibrators, especially to produce ultrasound (sound at a frequency higher than that which humans can hear). When the voltage across a piezoelectric crystal changes, the spacing between the two types of ions changes in response, producing motion of anything in contact with the crystal.

• **Ceramic Superconductors** The new high-temperature superconductors that you will read about in Chapter 6 are a ceramic material. However, before they can be used in the coils of powerful electromagnets, materials scientists and engineers will have to solve some very difficult problems. Making those high-temperature superconductors into wires is difficult because ceramics are so brittle.

• **Ceramic Magnets** When most people think of magnets, they think of iron. But experts in magnetics know that many of the most useful magnets are ceramics. In fact, the famous lodestone, the first known naturally magnetic material, is a ceramic called iron oxide. In electronics, a ceramic magnet can often have an advantage over a metallic magnet because it is an electrical insulator.

• **Ceramics in Construction and Household Use** Although these uses are generally not regarded as "high technology," we include bricks, tile, tableware, and plumbing fixtures among the many uses of versatile ceramic products. Ceramics are also used to create a variety of beautiful pieces of art.

Silica and Silicates Like carbon, silicon atoms have four bonding electrons. Oxygen atoms attach to two bonding electrons if they can. When silicon and oxygen combine, they can form either a molecule called silica or a silicate ion. Silica and silicates are the most important substances in the ceramics and glass industries.

In silica, or silicon dioxide, a silicon atom forms double bonds with two oxygen atoms. Silica is the main substance in sand, quartz, and other common minerals.

The silicate ion is made up of a silicon atom single-bonded to three oxygen atoms, plus two extra electrons that give it its electrical charge. The diagram shows that a silicate ion has one unbonded electron on its silicon atom, one oxy-gen atom with a spot where another bonding electron can connect, and one extra electron, indicated by a minus sign, on each of the other two oxygens.

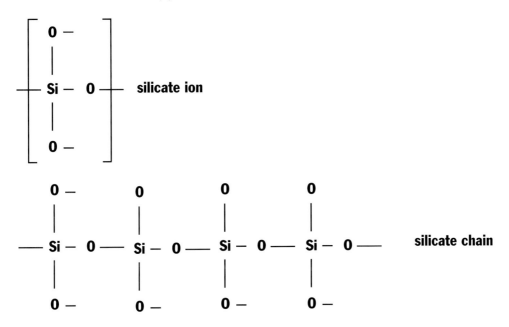

The diagram also shows that silicate ions can form long chains that resemble polymers. The silicate chain shown here and a polyethylene chain are similar in some ways and differ-ent in others. (See diagram on p. 66.) The main similarity is their ability to grow very long. The main difference is that the oxygen atoms at the top and bottom of the silicate chain have extra electrons that are ready to bond.

If they join with a metal ion, they form minerals known as silicates. If those electrons bond with an organic unit instead, the result is a silicate-based, rubbery polymer called a silicone. You have probably enjoyed playing with one kind of silicone called Silly Putty.®

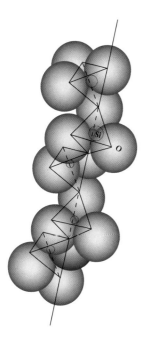

Silicate polymers (silicones) behave like interlocking chains of pyramid-shaped beads, while carbon-based linear polymers, like polyethylene, act like strings.

Another important difference between silicate polymers and hydrocarbon polymers is not obvious from the chain diagrams, because it is a three-dimensional effect. In hydrocarbon polymer molecules, the hydrogen atoms do not favor any particular arrangement, so the molecules behave much like strings.

In silicates, each silicon atom sits in the center of a tetrahedron, a four-sided solid like a pyramid with a triangular base, with oxygen atoms on each corner. The tetrahedrons are connected by so-called "bridging" oxygen atoms. Thus silicate chains resemble not strings but interlocking tetrahedral beads.

Furthermore, in silica and silicate materials, metal or silicon atoms link the silicate chains, forming a wonderful variety of either crystalline or amorphous arrangements of interconnected tetrahedra with a wide variety of properties. These minerals, including sand and quartz, are often referred to as network silicates. Many of them are quite interesting.

For example, the minerals mica and talc and natural clays are network silicates that form sheetlike structures. That explains why mica breaks easily into thin flakes and talc can be slippery. The pink mineral feldspar (potassium aluminum silicate), found in granite, is another network silicate.

Glassmaking begins with network silicates, usually silica in the form of sand. Silica is heated in the presence of "network modifiers," which are usually oxides like calcium oxide from heated calcium carbonate (lime) or sodium oxide from heated sodium carbonate (soda ash). These substances add metal ions and extra, nonbridging oxygen atoms. Those disrupt the network by reducing cross-linking between silicate chains and lower the melting point. Now when the material cools, it is an amorphous glass instead of a crystalline ceramic.

High-technology Glass Glass-making and -forming techniques have been developed over centuries. In that sense, it is an ancient art. But with the many high-tech applications of today, it is also a very modern technology. Here is a sampling of the exciting uses of that remarkable material called glass.

• Tempered Glass Your mental image of glass is probably that it is a material that breaks easily, like your neighbor's kitchen window that shattered when you hit an unexpectedly long home run. Yet glass can be made strong enough to be the walls of a modern metal and glass skyscraper. One way to strengthen glass is a process called tempering.

In that process, a piece of glass is cooled quickly on the surface while the inside remains hot. The outside then becomes like a solid bottle in the shape of the desired object, while the glass inside is still hot and soft. As the inside glass cools, it contracts and pulls inward on the bottle.

When the cooling is complete, the outside glass is permanently under an inward pulling stress, while the glass in the center is permanently stretched outward. Now imagine that a baseball—or perhaps even a bullet—hits the glass. The impact will stretch the outside and push the inside inward, opposite to the direction of the permanent internal forces of the glass. The inner forces will counteract the impact, and the projectile will bounce off without damage.

• **Glass Fibers for Insulation** People today are very conscious about the amount of energy they use. Insulating homes and buildings to minimize heat loss or to retain cool, conditioned air has become very important. The most widely used material for home and building insulation is a woolly material made of long, thin glass fibers.

• **High-tech Cookware** The microwave oven has become a very common item in the high-technology home. Microwave cooking needs pots and pans that do not absorb microwaves, so metal is out and glass is in!

In the microwave oven, the food gets hot but the pot does not. Because most people use microwave ovens, stove tops, and ordinary ovens at different times, glass manufacturers found a pot material that works in all three places. It does not melt at a temperature hot enough to turn a metal pot to soup. An early television commercial for that material showed a glass pot with a metal pot softening and bending inside it.

• **Optical Fibers for Medicine, Computers, and Communication** Of course, you can't be high-tech if you don't get into the medical, computer, and communication fields. Glass is at the forefront in all three areas because of "fiber optics."

Fiber optics refers to the use of carefully crafted fibers of glass that act as pipelines to carry light around corners and into areas that could never before be illuminated. The inside of the fiber is one type of glass and the outside is a different

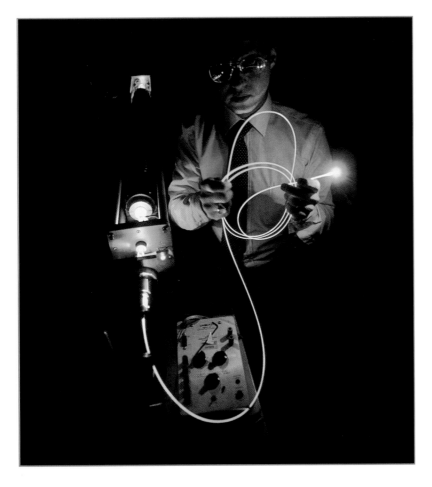

The first major use of fiberoptics was in many different kinds of medical tools to examine areas of the inside of the body that previously could only be seen during surgery. That breakthrough has saved many lives and eliminated many painful operations.

type. That design makes it possible to send a beam of light into one end of the fiber, have it bounce off the inside of the glass to follow twists and turns, and come out the end.

The first major use of fiberoptics was in many different kinds of medical tools to examine areas of the inside of the body that previously could only be seen during surgery. That breakthrough has saved many lives and eliminated many painful operations.

Today, the most exciting use of fiberoptics is in computation and communication. Information of one kind or another, from telephone voice signals to computer data, is turned into a digital code of on-off pulses of light. Specially designed optical fibers transmit those pulses farther than metal wires can. An optical fiber can carry four thousand times as much information as a copper cable of the same size. Its weight is so much less that a ship can now carry and lay a 3,000-mile (4,800-kilometer) undersea cable in a single trip. Formerly, several trips were needed. These improvements are a major reason for the great increase in use of telephone communications between people and computers and the decrease in cost of long-distance calls.

So new products of ceramic materials and glass enable us to travel into space, to heal our bodies, to cook our food, to conduct electricity, to compute, to communicate, and to deal with information in many ways that could only be imagined a few years ago. Who says the Stone Age is ancient history?

SUPER MATTER

Materials scientists and engineers are always looking to improve the properties of the Techno-Matter that they make. Sometimes, they discover ways to create matter with extreme properties. When they do, their reaction is likely to be, "Super!" Sometimes they even use "super" as part of the name of the material or property.

In the chapter about polymers, you read about superadhesives. In this chapter, you will read briefly about other super materials called composites. Most of this chapter tells a super story about a super phenomenon called superconductivity. Discoveries in that field have already led to three Nobel Prizes (the world's most respected award for scientific work) and may lead to more.

Ceramic materials are very hard. They can also withstand very high temperatures. But they are brittle; if you strike them with a hammer, they will shatter. Wouldn't it be super to have materials as strong or heat resistant as ceramics, yet flexible enough to bend instead of break?

COMPOSITES:
STRONG, LIGHT,
AND FLEXIBLE

71

Plastics and certain metals, such as magnesium and aluminum, are light in weight and easy to shape, but they are not very strong or heat resistant. Wouldn't it be super to have materials that are light, strong, heat-resistant, and easy to mold into whatever you want to make?

Such materials exist, and they are called composites. They are two very different materials put together so that the combination has the best properties of both.

Though composites are among today's most advanced materials, the first composite materials were invented in ancient times. Brick makers discovered that adding straw to hardening mud would stop cracks from growing. The resulting bricks had the strength of a ceramic but were less brittle.

Just as the ancient brick makers did, modern materials scientists and engineers look for ways to make Techno-Matter with super-strength and heat resistance but without brittleness. Instead of adding straw to mud, they are adding strong yet flexible materials, like graphite fibers, to today's advanced ceramics.

Materials scientists and engineers are also working on composites based on plastics and metals. They name composites for the main material, which serves as the supporting structure, or "matrix," of the composite.

You can find ceramic-matrix composites in lightweight yet powerful aircraft engines. For now, their cost is too high for automobile engines; but you may someday drive a car with a composite engine.

Because of its light but sturdy body of polymer-matrix (or plastic) composites, the ultralight *Voyager* airplane flew around the world in 1986 without refueling. Today's plastic composites save weight—and therefore save fuel—in automobiles and planes.

Because of its light but sturdy body of polymer-matrix (or plastic) composites, the ultralight Voyager airplane flew around the world in 1986 without refueling. Similar plastic composites today save weight—and therefore save fuel—in automobiles and airplanes.

You have already learned that steel is a multiphase alloy. It can be considered a metal-matrix composite with little regions of ceramic added to give it strength. Today's collection of Techno-Matter includes lighter-weight metal-matrix composites with greater strength and durability than steel.

Materials scientists are working on all sorts of composite Techno-Matter to change our everyday lives for the better. One everyday area in which composites have already made their mark is sports. The lightest, strongest, most flexible tennis racquets, vaulters' poles, and golf clubs all use composite materials.

SUPERCONDUCTIVITY: A SUPER STORY

Imagine a bowling alley that stretches around the world. You stand in front of the pins and launch a bowling ball in the opposite direction, right down the middle at a speed of 35 miles (55 kilometers) per hour. A month later your ball comes rolling toward the pins, still going 35 miles per hour. Your aim was perfect. "Strike!" you cheer. "What a super shot!"

Super, indeed! The ball circled the globe without slowing down one bit.

In 1911, Professor Heike Kamerlingh Onnes of the University of Leyden in the Netherlands had an experience like that in his laboratory. He was studying the properties of matter near "absolute zero," a temperature so cold that it can only be approached and never reached. One of the properties he investigated was electrical resistance in metals, such as mercury. (You may know mercury as a liquid metal, but it freezes solid when it gets very cold.)

Kamerlingh Onnes and other scientists reasoned that electrical resistance was caused by electrons bumping into vibrating atoms in the metal. The atoms would vibrate less at a low temperature than at a high one, so they expected that the resistance of mercury to decrease it cooled.

No one had studied temperatures as extreme as those that Kamerlingh Onnes could create in his laboratory—temperatures low enough to turn all the gases in the atmosphere to liquids. As the temperature decreased below the temperature of liquid nitrogen, the resistance of mercury continued its steady, gradual drop. Just barely below the temperature where helium turned to liquid, the resistance of his thin mercury thread dropped abruptly to zero. It was no longer an ordinary conductor of electricity, but a superconductor with no resistance at all!

It was an astonishing discovery. The atoms of the metal still vibrated, but the electrons flowed past them and between them without losing any energy. Either the electrons had stopped bumping into the atoms, or the electrons now left the collisions with exactly as much energy as they had when they hit the atoms in the first place. Neither idea made sense, but the experimental facts said it must be so.

Kamerlingh Onnes tested his discovery in many ways. He tried the same wire again and again. He tried different shapes of wires. No matter what, superconductivity always began when he cooled the mercury below the same temperature. He tried other metals, and found that some of them, too, became superconductors—tin at a slightly lower temperature and lead at a slightly higher one.

He made loops of superconducting wire, started current flowing in them, and came back hours later to find the currents still flowing as strongly as before. When he raised the temperature of the metal above where superconductivity started, the currents promptly died away.

In 1913 scientists honored Kamerlingh Onnes with the Nobel Prize in physics. None of those present at the awards ceremony knew that the "low-temperature" phenomenon of superconductivity would remain a "hot topic" throughout the rest of the twentieth century and into the twenty-first. Nor did they know that superconducting Techno-Matter would lead to lifesaving medical machines.

In the years following Kamerlingh Onnes's discovery, many scientists searched for materials that became superconducting at higher temperatures. Others searched for a theory that explained the phenomenon. Still other scientists and engineers imagined what they might build with such materi-

Kamerlingh Onnes's careful work demonstrated that superconductivity was real, although it would be nearly half a century before anyone could explain it.

als, like superconducting wire coiled into powerful electro-magnets that never got hot.

Progress in the theory was slow. Finally, in 1957, John Bardeen (who had just received the 1956 Nobel Prize in physics for inventing the transistor), Leon N. Cooper, and John Robert Schrieffer wrote a famous article that explained what happened to electrons in superconductors. Their theory, known as the BCS theory after the initials of their last names, explained that each moving electron has a partner, with which it forms a "Cooper pair."

The Cooper pairs travel through the crystal lattice, and the lattice, like a plucked violin string, vibrates. When one member of the Cooper pair bumps into a vibrating atom, it gives up some energy, not to the atom but to the vibration as a whole. The vibration, now stronger, immediately transfers its newly gained energy to the other electron of the pair.

Then the process reverses. The second electron loses its just-gained energy to the vibration, and the first one regains it. The two paired electrons continue to exchange that energy, never losing any as they travel through the lattice. They ride through the lattice together—without electrical resistance—on a microscopic sound wave.

For this remarkable theory, Bardeen, Cooper, and Schrieffer received the 1972 Nobel Prize in physics, the second awarded for superconductivity. Their theory not only explained superconductivity in metals but it also suggested directions for other scientists to look for new superconducting Techno-Matter. They hoped to find a material that was superconducting at high enough temperatures that expensive liquid helium cooling would no longer be needed.

For a while, there was steady progress toward higher temperatures. Around the time of the BCS Nobel Prize, scientists had made alloys that were superconducting at a temperature nearly one third of the temperature of liquid nitrogen. Then the progress suddenly ended; it seemed no one could go further. Some scientists even wrote articles explaining why superconductivity was unlikely at higher temperatures, and many laboratories stopped working on it.

A few scientists kept working on superconductivity. Even if they could not raise the temperature at which it would occur, they could learn more about the electrical properties of materials. Among those who persisted were Georg Bednorz and K. Alex Müller at the IBM Corporation's research laboratory in Zurich, Switzerland.

Bednorz and Müller read about other scientists' research that showed unexpectedly high superconducting temperatures in some nonmetallic materials. The temperatures were far below the record, but far above where theory had predicted them to be. To them, those results were nature's hints to a path toward superconductivity at higher temperatures—and they decided to follow it. In late 1986, they reported superconductivity in a ceramic, lanthanum barium copper oxide, at nearly halfway to the temperature of liquid nitrogen, a new record.

That discovery set off a flurry of activity in laboratories all over the world. Scientists worked night and day; some even slept on cots in their labs. Everyone wanted to be the first to discover superconductivity above liquid nitrogen temperature, or, with enormous good fortune, at room temperature.

In 1987, Professor Paul C. W. Chu of the University of Houston announced that he and his associate M. K. Wu of the University of Alabama had discovered that yttrium barium copper oxide was superconducting at a temperature 16ºC (about 30ºF) above the temperature where nitrogen becomes liquid. Though the superconducting temperature was still −180ºC (or −292ºF), Chu's announcement spread the excitement beyond the labs and onto the front pages of newspapers around the world.

That discovery, the papers reported, marked the beginning of a new era in superconductivity—and perhaps a new era in technology itself. No longer did all superconductors require cooling in expensive liquid helium; now some could be cooled in liquid nitrogen instead.

Since liquid nitrogen is relatively inexpensive (it costs about as much as milk) engineers and businesspeople who heard the announcement began to dream of the many new ways that these new superconducting materials might be used. They imagined superconductors in advanced computer chips, in high-speed trains that run with little friction on a magnetic cushion, and in wires that could carry electricity for miles without the usual loss of energy.

Some of the dreams required room-temperature superconductivity; but in the excitement, that temperature no longer seemed out of reach. In 1987 and 1988, new temperature records appeared almost weekly, as did new types of "high-temperature superconductors," as they came to be known. By the time the field began to settle down, the high temperature record stood at a still frigid -148°C (or -234°F), and Bednorz and Müller had been awarded the 1987 Nobel Prize in physics, the third one given for work in superconductivity.

The Future of Superconductivity Though the excitement of the late 1980s has ended, for scientists and engineers, the best work still lies ahead. Can they make useful devices from this new class of superconducting Techno-Matter? Will they need another theoretical breakthrough like BCS theory to understand the latest discoveries? Will other diligent scientists like Bednorz and Müller discover room-temperature superconductors? Or have we reached a real limit this time?

Even if room-temperature superconductors are discovered, will we be able to use them in practical devices? For that matter, can we do anything useful with the latest "high-temperature superconductors"? Although those superconductors have generated enormous interest, they have had little practical use.

Why? Part of the reason is that they, like other ceramics, are hard and brittle. Unlike metallic superconductors, they are very difficult to form into wires. Also, if you try to force too much current through them or expose them to a strong magnetic field, they lose their superconductivity.

Can materials scientists and engineers solve those problems, making those superconductors more flexible, able to carry more current, and able to function in a powerful magnetic field? They are making steady progress by changing the microstructure and measuring what happens.

To use high-temperature superconductors in computer chips and other electronic devices, engineers think not only of tiny superconducting wires, but also of superconducting "thin films." If you were to make a layer of superconducting material only a few atoms thick, or even a few hundred atoms thick, how would its properties differ from a thick, solid piece? Could you take advantage of some unusual properties of thin films to make a useful device?

Superconductors in Use Although the future of high-temperature superconductors is uncertain, low-temperature superconductivity already has its place in modern technology. Today's most powerful magnets are electromagnets made from superconducting wire. The materials from which

This levitating magnet is floating freely above a nitrogen-cooled cylindrical specimen of a superconducting ceramic, thus demonstrating the Meissner effect. The vapor is from liquid nitrogen, which maintains the ceramic within its superconducting temperature range.

that wire is made are the result of years of study of the properties and microstructure of superconducting metals and alloys. Although liquid helium cooling is expensive, the power of these magnets makes them very valuable for certain applications and well worth the cost.

For example, Magnetic Resonance Imaging (MRI) gives physicians detailed pictures of their patients' internal organs in ways that X rays cannot. Furthermore, MRI carries less risk of long-term harm to the patients' health. Without powerful superconducting magnets, MRI would be less effective and quite limited.

Superconducting magnets are also important for particle accelerators, which scientists are using to unlock the secrets of particles even smaller than atoms. Another use for superconducting magnets is in "maglev" (magnetic levitation) trains. These futuristic transportation systems are already in use in Germany and Japan, and several American cities are considering maglev. Maglev trains use electromagnets to lift them toward the top of a T-shaped rail, and some train designs call for superconducting magnets.

You may have seen pictures or demonstrations of a different kind of magnetic levitation of superconductors. The picture on page 80 shows a small magnet floating in liquid nitrogen above a piece of high-temperature superconductor. Like iron, the superconductor becomes a magnet when placed in a magnetic field. But unlike iron, it becomes magnetized in the opposite direction from the field, and thus repels the magnet instead of attracting it. This behavior exists in some other materials, but only weakly. It is called "diamagnetism." A superconductor, however, is a "perfect diamagnet," developing a repelling field as strong as the one that magnetizes it.

This effect, called the Meissner effect after the scientist who discovered it in the 1930s, is considered the proof that a material is truly a superconductor and not just something with exceptionally low resistance. Because of the Meissner effect, people have thought about devices that use superconductors for magnetic levitation or as a magnetic shield; but so far, nothing practical has come of it.

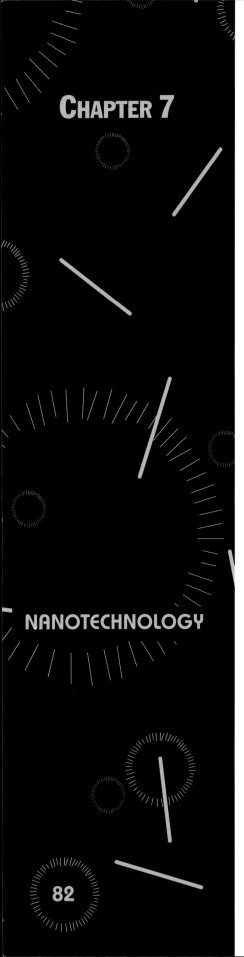

CHAPTER 7

FUTURE MATTER

What Techno-Matter will future materials scientists and engineers discover and create? That prediction is both hard and easy. The easy part is saying that materials will keep getting better. The hard part is predicting which materials will be the most important for technology.

Still, a book like this is not complete without predictions. Its final pages contain a small sampling of the many possibilities that lie ahead in the world of Future Matter.

What makes Techno-Matter work? By now you know the answer: To understand a material, you start with microstructure.

Wouldn't it be amazing if you could make whatever microstructure you would like, atom by atom? With the tools in the most advanced materials science laboratories, some scientists can almost do that.

Although people cannot see atoms with ordinary microscopes, the newest tools of materials science can produce images that show individual atoms and the shape of single molecules. Some instruments don't just "see" atoms; they can move them around, one at a time.

Using these advanced instruments, scientists can make materials with amazing properties. The only limits are the laws of nature and their imaginations. When they make structures as small as a few atoms, they often call the process "nanotechnology."

The word makes doubly good sense. In Chapter 3, you were introduced to the term microfabrication with its metric prefix *micro-*, meaning a millionth of a meter. The next smaller metric prefix, "nano-," means one billionth, and a nanometer is the size of a few atoms.

At Rice University in Houston, Texas, scientists under the leadership of Professor Richard Smalley are studying a promising class of Techno-Matter with a whimsical name. As often happens in science, the discovery of these materials began with a surprise in the laboratory.

In the 1980s, Smalley had developed an instrument to study cluster chemistry: chemical reactions between small numbers of atoms. One day, he put carbon in the apparatus, vaporized it, and got the surprise of his scientific career. His enthusiasm bubbles whenever he describes what happened:

> We discovered that in carbon vapor. . ., as you cool it down, [sixty carbon atoms] spontaneously come together to form this object. . . . Sixty is such a large number. You think that, well, if sixty is special, then probably fifty-nine's not bad, and fifty-eight, and sixty-one, and sixty-two. But uh-uh; just nothin', then sixty, then nothin' again.

It's almost as though the apparatus reached out with its hand and grabbed us and said, "I'll bet you can't figure me out!" That was really stunning. . . .

Within a day we realized that there's a special answer: [The sixty atoms] take the structure of a soccer ball. . . . What is amazing is that's the *only* possible answer. Just from [mathematics], there is no other arrangement of sixty atoms that is an explanation for that one piece of data.

As discoverers of the molecule, Dr. Smalley and his colleagues had the privilege of naming it. They called it "buckminsterfullerene" after the famous architect R. Buckminster Fuller, who designed buildings based on the same "geodesic dome" structure as the molecule. Soon, the sixty-carbon molecule—and similar, elongated molecules with larger numbers of carbon atoms that were discovered not long afterwards—had a nickname: "buckyballs."

The arrangement of carbon atoms in buckyballs is similar to the chicken-wire arrangement of graphite, except that one wire in some of the hexagons is cut out and the graphite sheet bends into a ball. At first, Smalley's group could make only small amounts of buckminsterfullerene, and buckyballs remained only a laboratory curiosity. Then another group of scientists accidentally discovered how to make a kind of soot full of the curious carbon balls.

After that, the molecule caught the attention of scientists all over the world, and not just because of its funny name. They realized that the ball-shaped carbon molecules could arrange themselves into an oversized crystal lattice.

That lattice—or the molecules themselves—could act as cages for other atoms. It was perfect for materials science,

because its microstructure could be changed in controlled ways. Some Bucky-Matter was superconducting; other Bucky-Matter had interesting magnetic properties. Soon hundreds of laboratories around the world were making soot, purifying it, adding other atoms, and studying the results.

In Dr. Smalley's laboratories, scientists found even more interesting kinds of Bucky-Matter, such as long tubelike carbon molecules, like rolled-up graphite sheets. Made into fibers, they might be hundreds of times stronger than steel. With metal atoms down the middle, they could be tiny wires with very low electrical resistance—not superconductors, but the next best thing. The resistance of those bucky-wires is hundreds of times smaller than the best metals.

Because of his work with Bucky-Matter, Dr. Smalley won the Nobel Prize in chemistry in 1996; but he isn't satisfied yet. As he puts it, "Bucky still hasn't got a job." No one has found a way to make practical use of any of the members of this large and fascinating family of materials, although in late 2000, scientists at the Lawrence Berkeley National Laboratory announced the creation of the tiniest transistor ever built. It is a single buckeyball atom sandwiched between gold electrodes. So, if you're looking for the next Techno-Matter breakthrough, it wouldn't be a bad idea to hang around a Bucky-lab, where interesting things are beginning to happen.

THIN FILMS, INTERFACES, AND MULTILAYERS

Strange as it may seem, even a perfect crystal is imperfect in a very important way. If you could stand anywhere in a perfect crystal, you would see exactly the same pattern. But that can be true only if the crystal goes on forever. Real crystals end at their surfaces.

Atoms at the surface have neighbors in one direction but not the opposite. That makes the properties of the surface of a material very different from the properties of the inside. That makes thin films very interesting to materials scientists and engineers, because they have a large fraction of their atoms near the surface. The thinner a film is, the more unusual its properties.

Thin films are also interesting, because they contain so little material that people can afford to make them out of very scarce substances. It usually costs much more to buy and run the equipment to make a thin film than to buy the material that it contains.

Thin films are often only the starting point. When two different surfaces come together, they form an interface. The properties of each surface depends on the atoms of the other one. The properties of interfaces are often even more unusual than the properties of surfaces. Thus scientists who study surfaces often study interfaces as well.

Many future breakthroughs are likely to come from surface and interface studies, but some scientists aren't stopping there. They are letting their imaginations consider what would happen if a material is made up of thin films of different types stacked up layer by layer. The properties could change dramatically if the thickness of the layers were to change. These multilayer structures are likely to be the source of many future breakthrough materials.

MANUFACTURING IN A WEIGHTLESS ENVIRONMENT

Gravity is often a problem in manufacturing. An object inside an orbiting satellite is still influenced by the Earth's gravity, but it seems to be weightless because both it and its sur-

roundings are falling at exactly the same rate. (They don't fall to Earth because they are also moving parallel to the surface, which curves away beneath them as fast as they are falling.) Thus an artificial satellite is a place where people do experiments on the effects of weightlessness.

A number of space flights have included experiments in making high-purity materials with more perfect crystals. As people establish permanent orbiting laboratories, materials science and engineering have high priority. Breakthroughs in space-made Techno-Matter are not only likely, but expected.

IMITATING NATURE

Though most materials scientists and engineers try to do what nature cannot, a few study the materials nature has made that we cannot yet duplicate. They call their field of work "biomimetics," because they are mimicking the

One of the subjects of biomimetics research is the adhesive by which barnacles attach themselves to the rather slippery skin of a whale.

processes of life. One of the most important is spider silk because of its light weight and high strength.

Other subjects of biomimetics research include the springy material in the hinge of a fly's wing and the adhesive that barnacles use to attach themselves to ships or whales. The shell of the abalone is a natural composite. Strong but light materials in wood and the external skeletons of insects also provide plenty of ideas for new artificial materials.

BIOMATERIALS

Artificial body parts and organs are taking their place among the great advances in modern medicine. One of the greatest challenges in designing an artificial part is deciding what materials to use in making it. The so-called biomaterials must work well with living tissue for a lifetime. Materials scientists and engineers will be hard at work to find materials that will do the job of the original body part and will neither harm nor be harmed by the body.

TECHNO-MATTER AND YOU

So what lies ahead for Techno-Matter? No one can make specific predictions, but everyone who works in materials science and engineering is sure that there will be more excitement of all kinds. They can expect a lifetime of breakthroughs, discoveries, surprises, inventions, and rewards, providing great benefits for the rest of us.

Techno-Matter will offer a wealth of areas to explore, and that exploration will involve many people with many different talents: scientists, engineers, computer scientists, technicians, writers, and businesspeople, to name a few. You may work in the field, but even if you don't, your life will be affected by it. You live in a world of high technology, and technology has always been based on the materials at hand.

We humans have come a long way since we first discovered what we can do with the materials of nature, and we've come a long way since we first discovered how to make our own. Now that we can see atoms and move them around, where will we go from here?

No one knows the answer, but it will surely be lots of fun to find out where Techno-Matter will take us—perhaps to Mars and beyond!

GLOSSARY

ABSOLUTE ZERO - A temperature so cold that it is impossible to reach, although it can be approached. Scientists usually measure low temperatures in the number of Celsius degrees above absolute zero or kelvins.

ALLOY - A material that results from mixing two or more metals. It has properties that are often significantly different from the metals that go into it.

AMORPHOUS — A type of microstructure in which the atoms of the material are not arranged in any regular pattern. Glass is the best-known amorphous material.

ANNEALING — A process in which a material, especially an alloy or glass, is heated to just below its melting point and held there for a length of time during which the microstructure can change significantly through the movement of atoms within the material.

ATOM — The smallest unit of matter that can be identified as a chemical element.

BCS THEORY — A theory proposed by physicists John Bardeen, Leon N. Cooper, and John Robert Schrieffer that explains the phenomenon of superconductivity in certain materials.

BIOMATERIALS — Artificial materials designed to perform well within a living body, such as long-lasting artificial joints and organs.

BIOMIMETICS — The creation of artificial materials based on biological materials with unusual and important properties, such as spider silk, fly-wing hinges, and the adhesive made by barnacles.

BOND — A connection that forms between two atoms in a molecule or a crystal.

BORT, or BORTZ — The name of the author of this book, and coincidentally the word used to describe a quantity of low-quality diamonds and diamond fragments that are used in industry for polishing or grinding.

BRONZE AGE — The period of human history immediately following the Stone Age, during which the discovery of the alloy bronze revolutionized civilization by making possible many new or improved tools, implements, and weapons.

BUCKYBALLS — The nickname given to buckminsterfullerene and similar carbon-based molecules.

BUCKMINSTERFULLERENE — A molecule in the shape of a soccer ball made of sixty carbon atoms. It was the first of a potentially very important family of molecules discovered in a cluster chemistry experiment. Its name honors architect R. Buckminster Fuller, who created build-

ings in the shape of geodesic domes, which have the same arrangement of pentagons and hexagons as this molecule.

CERAMICS — A class of materials that are chemical compounds of metals or semimetals and nonmetals. Ceramics are generally light, strong, and resistant to corrosion and heat. They are also usually quite brittle.

CLUSTER CHEMISTRY — A technique that relies on the reaction of a small number of atoms. The potentially important family of materials related to "buckminsterfullerene" was first discovered in a cluster chemistry experiment.

COLD-WORKING — The process of applying mechanical stresses to a material, usually a metal or alloy, without heating it. Cold-working can harden a material by changing its microstructure, mainly by moving its dislocations and creating new ones.

COMPOSITES — A class of human-made multiphase materials in which the main phase (the matrix) is either ceramic, metal, or polymer, and the second phase is often a fiber like graphite or a tiny particle. The additional material is added to lessen the effect of an undesirable property, such as brittleness, in the matrix material.

COMPOUND — A substance whose molecules are all the same.

CONDUCTIVITY — The ability of a material to permit an electric current (electrical conductivity) or heat (thermal conductivity) to pass through it.

CROSS-LINKING — The formation of chemical bonds between two widely separated units of a polymer molecule, producing a three-dimensional microstructure and major changes in properties.

CRYSTAL — An orderly, repeating arrangement of the atoms or molecules of a material that often results in its ability to be cut into pieces with smooth faces and sharp edges or to form naturally into such pieces.

DEFECT, or IMPERFECTION — A region of a crystal in which the orderly arrangement of its atoms or molecules is disrupted.

DIODE — An electrical or electronic device that permits the flow of electrical current in only one direction.

DISLOCATION — A crystal defect in which the atomic planes are slightly offset from each other.

DOPING — The controlled introduction of an impurity into a material. Doping is especially important for creating semiconductor devices with desirable properties.

ELECTROLYSIS — A process in which the passage of an electric current through a liquid reverses the chemical reaction that caused a compound to form. Aluminum is produced by electrolysis of molten aluminum oxide.

ELECTRON — One of the very light, negatively charged particles that form a cloud around the nucleus of an atom. Electrons are responsible for the bonding of atoms into molecules and crystals. In metals and other solids, they are the particles responsible for electrical conductivity.

ELECTRONICS — A branch of technology based on the ability to control the flow of signals or energy by controlling the motion of electrons. Semiconductor technology has revolutionized human civilization through the development of electronic devices with many new capabilities.

ELEMENT — A substance whose atoms are all the same.

GLASS — An amorphous material generally made from silicon dioxide along with few other substances. Scientists sometimes use the term glass to describe any amorphous material.

GRAIN — One of many small crystalline regions of a material made up of many such regions.

HIGH-TECHNOLOGY — A term used to describe the most advanced technology of the present time.

HOLE — An bonding site in a crystal that is missing an electron. It acts as if it is a positive charge, since electrons are attracted to it.

HOT-WORKING — The process of applying mechanical stresses to a material, usually a metal or alloy, while heating it. Hot-working changes the properties and microstructure of a material by causing the motion of its defects or by creating new ones.

IMPERFECTION — See DEFECT.

IMPURITY — A crystal defect consisting of an atom of a type that is not part of the normal chemical makeup of the crystal, such as an atom of aluminum in a crystal of silicon.

INCLUSION — A small region of a crystal that is different chemically or in crystal structure from the material surrounding it. Inclusions of graphite diminish the gem-quality value of a diamond.

INDUSTRIAL REVOLUTION — The recent period of human history in which the development of steam power and advances in steel-making led to great changes in industry and society.

INSULATOR — A material that has a low conductivity. It can be used to protect a person or device from the flow of heat or electricity.

INTEGRATED CIRCUIT (IC) — A device that contains a large number of transistors or other electrical components on a single piece of semiconductor material. It is produced by micro-fabrication techniques.

INTERFACE — The region where two different surfaces meet.

INTERSTITIAL — A crystal defect consisting of an atom in between normal crystal lattice sites.

IRON AGE — The period of human history during which the spread of knowledge of how to make iron gradually led to the replacement of most bronze items with iron items. Since iron ore is much more plentiful than copper (the main material in bronze), this led to significant changes in civilization.

LATTICE — A regular pattern that is the basis for the crystal structure of a solid. In a perfect crystal, each lattice site is occupied by an atom of a particular type.

MATERIAL — A substance out of which an object is made.

MATERIALS SCIENCE — A new science that developed in the second half of the twentieth century from the parts of the older sciences of metallurgy, chemistry, and physics that relate to the microstructure of materials.

MATERIALS ENGINEERING — The application of materials science to create new materials with desirable properties.

METAL — A material in which its atoms are held together by bonds formed by electrons shared by all the atoms. Metals are usually shiny, hard (when solid), and excellent conductors of heat and electricity.

MICROFABRICATION — A collection of techniques used to make devices of microscopic size, for example the many transistors on an integrated circuit. Many microfabrication techniques are based on precision methods of photography.

MICROSTRUCTURE — The arrangement of the atoms and molecules of a material, including crystal structure, defects, and differences in chemical composition.

MOLECULE — A particular combination of atoms that stays together. For example, a water molecule is a combination of two hydrogen atoms and one oxygen atom.

MULTILAYERS — Artificial materials made by stacking different thin films on top of each other.

MULTIPHASE — Having a microstructure made up of mixed regions with different compositions, crystal structures, or both. Steel is a very important multiphase material.

NANOTECHNOLOGY — Technology that depends on creating and manipulating structures as small as a nanometer in size, the extent of a few atoms.

NUCLEUS — The central portion of the atom that contains most of its mass. It consists of a certain number of positively charged protons and electrically neutral neutrons.

OPTICAL FIBER — A long, narrow filament of glass that transmits a light beam much as an electric wire carries an electrical current.

ORE — A material from which a metal can be extracted.

PIEZOELECTRIC — Having the property of producing a pulse of electric current when stressed or responding to a pulse of electric current by changing shape. Piezoelectric materials can be used as pressure sensors or to produce high-frequency mechanical vibrations from electric currents.

POLYMER - A molecule that consists of many repetitions of the same unit of a particular atomic arrangement, forming a "macromolecule." Plastics and synthetic fabrics are among the most important materials made of polymers.

PROPERTY — A quality of, or the way a particular material or substance behaves under particular conditions. For example: density; mechanical hardness; conductivity of heat or electricity; magnetic behavior; response to or interaction with light, sound, or pressure.

QUENCHING — The technique of rapidly cooling a material to produce a desired microstructure.

REFRACTORY — Able to withstand extremely high temperatures. One major application of ceramics is as refractory materials.

SEMICONDUCTOR — A material which has an electrical conductivity that is very sensitive to the presence of impurities. Careful doping of semiconductors is the basis of the electronics industry.

SILICATE — A material containing the silicate ion (a silicon atom, three oxygen atoms, and two electrons). Many important ceramics are silicates.

SMELTING — A process to remove a metal from its ore by heating in air, sometimes requiring the addition of another substance.

STACKING FAULT — A crystal defect in which a plane of atoms is missing or in the wrong sequence.

STONE AGE — A very early period of human development that began about two million years ago and continued until about seven thousand years before the present. During most of the Stone Age, people made tools from natural materials, such as stone. In the last few thousand years of the Stone Age, they discovered how to make ceramics, the first human-made materials, from clays.

SUPERCONDUCTOR — A material that conducts electricity perfectly without loss of energy. To date, superconductivity has only been observed at temperatures far below room temperature.

TECHNOLOGY — A device, tool, or machine used to manipulate, create, or transform an artificial or natural object, or the creation of a such a device or tool.

THIN FILM — A material made in the form of a thin coating of a substance on top of another substance. A thin film may have unusual and valuable properties because the molecules at the surface of a material behave differently from those in the interior. Thin-film materials are an important and growing area of technology.

TRANSISTOR — An electronic device that can behave as a controllable switch or an amplifier. It is made by careful doping of a semiconductor. The invention of the transistor is generally considered to have led to great technological and societal changes.

VACANCY — A crystal defect in which a lattice site is empty rather than containing an atom as it would if the crystal were perfect.

FOR FURTHER INFORMATION

Materials science and technology have always been underappreciated fields. Almost all of the books and articles on the subject are written for advanced college students and research professionals. Not many years ago, I was one of those researchers, but I also liked writing for young readers.

The more I learned about materials science and engineering in my work, the more I realized that young readers needed to know more about those fields. In 1989 I worked with a noted professor to write an article called "Materials Science" for *The New Book of Knowledge* young peoples' encyclopedia. That article led directly to my first book on this topic, called *Superstuff! Materials That Have Changed Our Lives* (Franklin Watts, 1990). It is for more advanced readers and presents more details than this book about the science of materials. If you're ready for more science when you finish *Techno-Matter*, then *Superstuff!* is a good book to read next.

For a different approach to advanced materials, read the January 1997 issue of *Odyssey* magazine, which uses Superstuff! as its theme. Its articles discuss mainly the way people use artificial materials and the way people are likely to use them in the future.

Another excellent book for learning more about materials science is *Stuff: The Materials the World Is Made Of* by Ivan Amato (Basic Books, 1997). It is written for adults, but it may be within your reach after you finish *Techno-Matter* and *Superstuff!*

You might also enjoy *The Substance of Civilization* by Stephen L. Sass (Arcade, 1998). Also written for adults, it looks at the role of new materials in each major period of human history "from the Stone Age to the Age of Silicon." It is less scientific than either *Superstuff!* or *Stuff*, but it will help you understand how important human-made materials have always been in the lives of everyday people.

Information on-line is always changing very rapidly, but one Web site will always be a good place to start—The Materials Research Society (http://www.mrs.org) is an outstanding professional organization. As this book was going to press, the MRS Web site had a great set of educational links about materials at its "Materials Gateway" page. Clicking on the question, "What is Materials Research?" took users to the links page http://www.mrs.org/gateway/matsci.html.

I will keep a link to that page (or one like it) on my Web site, http://www.fredbortz.com. Go first to the "Books by Dr. Fred" Web page and from there to the Web page for *Techno-Matter* to find that link.

INDEX